and

LIVING
THE LECTIONARY

LIVING
THE LECTIONARY
LINKS TO LIFE AND LITERATURE

YEAR A

GEOFF WOOD

LITURGY
TRAINING
PUBLICATIONS

Acknowledgments

We are grateful to the many publishers and authors who have given permission to include their work. Every effort has been made to determine the ownership of all texts and to make proper arrangement for their use. We will gladly correct in future editions any oversight or error that is brought to our attention.

"Neither Out Far Nor In Deep" from THE POETRY OF ROBERT FROST edited by Edward Connery Lathem. Copyright 1936 by Robert Frost, © 1964 by Lesley Frost Ballantine, © 1969 by Henry Holt and Company. Reprinted by permission of Henry Holt and Company, LLC.

"Primary Wonder" by Denise Levertov, from SANDS OF THE WELL, copyright © 1994, 1995, 1996 by Denise Levertov. Reprinted by permission of New Directions Publishing Corp.

LIVING THE LECTIONARY: LINKS TO LIFE AND LITERATUARE, YEAR A © 2004 Archdiocese of Chicago: Liturgy Training Publications, 1800 North Hermitage Avenue, Chicago IL 60622-1101; 1-800-933-1800, fax 1-800-933-7094, e-mail orders@ltp.org. All rights reserved. See our website at www.ltp.org.

This book was edited by Margaret Brennan. Kris Fankhouser was the production editor. The design is by Anna Manhart, and the typesetting was done by Kari Nicholls in Minion.

Printed in Canada.

Library of Congress Control Number: 2004109031

ISBN 1-56854-523-1
LIVLA

Contents

Season of Advent

First Sunday of Advent   2

Second Sunday of Advent   4

Second Sunday of Advent, Option   6

Third Sunday of Advent   8

Fourth Sunday of Advent   10

Season of Christmas

The Nativity of the Lord, Mass at Midnight   12

The Holy Family of Jesus, Mary, and Joseph   15

Epiphany   17

The Baptism of the Lord   19

Season of Lent

First Sunday of Lent   22

Second Sunday of Lent   24

Third Sunday of Lent   26

Fourth Sunday of Lent   28

Fifth Sunday of Lent   30

Palm Sunday of the Lord's Passion   32

Passiontide   34

Season of Easter

The Vigil in the Holy Night of Easter   36

Second Sunday of Easter   39

Second Sunday of Easter, Option   41

Third Sunday of Easter   43

Fourth Sunday of Easter   45

Fifth Sunday of Easter   47

Sixth Sunday of Easter   49

Seventh Sunday of Easter, Feast of the Ascension   51

Pentecost Sunday   53

Pentecost Sunday, Topical   55

Ordinary Time

The Most Holy Trinity   58

The Most Holy Body and Blood of Christ   60

The Most Holy Body and Blood of Christ, Topical   62

Second Sunday in Ordinary Time   64

Third Sunday in Ordinary Time   66

Fourth Sunday in Ordinary Time 68

Fifth Sunday in Ordinary Time 70

Sixth Sunday in Ordinary Time 73

Seventh Sunday in Ordinary Time 75

Eighth Sunday in Ordinary Time 77

Ninth Sunday in Ordinary Time 79

Tenth Sunday in Ordinary Time 81

Tenth Sunday in Ordinary Time, Topical 83

Eleventh Sunday in Ordinary Time 85

Twelfth Sunday in Ordinary Time 87

Twelfth Sunday in Ordinary Time, Topical 90

Thirteenth Sunday in Ordinary Time 92

Fourteenth Sunday in Ordinary Time 94

Fifteenth Sunday in Ordinary Time 96

Sixteenth Sunday in Ordinary Time 98

Seventeenth Sunday in Ordinary Time 99

Eighteenth Sunday in Ordinary Time 101

Nineteenth Sunday in Ordinary Time 103

Twentieth Sunday in Ordinary Time 105

Twenty-first Sunday in Ordinary Time 107

Twenty-second Sunday in Ordinary Time 109

Twenty-third Sunday in Ordinary Time 111

Twenty-third Sunday in Ordinary Time, Topical 114

Twenty-fourth Sunday in Ordinary Time 116

Twenty-fifth Sunday in Ordinary Time 118

Twenty-sixth Sunday in Ordinary Time 120

Twenty-seventh Sunday in Ordinary Time 122

Twenty-eighth Sunday in Ordinary Time 124

Twenty-ninth Sunday in Ordinary Time 126

Thirtieth Sunday in Ordinary Time 128

Thirty-first Sunday in Ordinary Time 130

Thirty-second Sunday in Ordinary Time 132

Thirty-third Sunday in Ordinary Time 134

Last Sunday in Ordinary Time, Our Lord Jesus Christ the King 136

The Commemoration of All the Faithful Departed 138

Secular Holidays

Mother's Day 140

Memorial Day 142

Father's Day 144

Endnotes *147*

FIRST SUNDAY OF ADVENT

Isaiah 2:1–5

They Shall Beat Their Swords into Plowshares

It took the destruction of September 11, 2001, to awaken me to an important but somewhat forgotten tenet of our Catholic tradition. Why was that? After all, for decades the media had confronted me with daily images of destruction: world wars, genocide, assassinations, nuclear threat. Add to that the ever more explicit fictional violence produced by Hollywood and, if destruction is what I needed to wake me up, one may wonder how I could have remained asleep so long.

But there was something about that September 11 that snapped me out of it—something so cold-heartedly violent, so self-righteously vindictive that the word "evil" returned to my vocabulary. And then I began to recall how destructiveness has been the bane of human nature ever since Cain killed Abel and his descendant Lamech avenged himself seventy times seven times—a record that has been surpassed in modern times and certainly was on that day. The thought of how the spores of this destructive tendency infect us all, commencing with little things like snide remarks, depressed me.

But how could I remain depressed when simultaneously, with the collapse of those twin towers, I beheld so moving a display of human intimacy and solidarity—how people, normally insulated from each other by personal preoccupations, suddenly became kinfolk, ready to comfort, to assist, to lay down their lives to save? How could I remain depressed when, no sooner are we confronted by the worst human nature is capable of, the Holy Spirit goes so quickly to work to bring out the best we are capable of?

There was something else, however, that hit me as I looked at the grotesque ruins of the World Trade Center. Its destruction began to revive my appreciation of all that is constructive in human nature. I began to look around and notice things like the New York skyline, the Golden Gate Bridge, the shops around the Plaza, the house I live in (made by somebody I don't even know)—and automobiles, shovels, salt-shakers, wedding rings, the pavement laid by vulnerable highway workers, markets loaded with produce gathered by unseen hands. I began to appreciate the mechanics at my local service station, my physician, the landscape people, the poets, the trash collectors, the long series of people who, when I flip a switch, flood my home with light and warmth. And the ancient tenet of our faith, our dogma of creation, came back to me with an importance I had too long ignored.

Too often we go about our work for trivial reasons: to make money, to keep busy, to achieve awards, to pursue mere personal satisfaction, forgetting that every constructive thing we do is somehow related to the creation of a world, the reconstruction of Eden. We forget that the genealogy of every positive product of human labor, be it a bottle cap or lampshade or garden or the clothes we wear or a budget or counseling session, can be traced back to the God who began it all when he said, "Let there be light!" Saint Paul confirms this when he says so beautifully in his letter to the Romans: "All creation is groaning in labor pains even until now; and not only that. But we ourselves, who have the first fruits of the Spirit, we also groan within" to bring forth something wonderful.

Labor! Advent is that season of the year when Mother Church, along with Mary, will once more go into labor to bring forth Christ, to beget a world in which life-sustaining tools like plowshares and pruning hooks at last supplant swords, spears, and weapons of mass destruction. What better time then to remind ourselves that our own constructive labor, however unheralded it may be, contributes to God's age-old effort to lift humanity out of primeval chaos, to fashion a world in which self-righteous destruction will have no more currency—"nor shall they train for war again."

SECOND SUNDAY OF ADVENT

Isaiah 11:1–10, Charles Dickens, Frank Norris

The Peaceable Kingdom

The Advent readings this year include a dream of the prophet Isaiah anticipating a day when "the wolf shall be the guest of the lamb and the leopard will lie down with the kid; the calf and the young lion will graze together"—in other words, a day when animals will no longer relate to each other as predator and prey but live in playful harmony. And no! Isaiah's not anticipating our modern zoo where an appearance of neighborly relationship takes place—thanks to iron bars! As a matter of fact, he's not even talking about animals literally; he's talking metaphorically about human beings who have been known to relate to one another as predator and prey.

It was Charles Darwin who startled our complacently "civilized" world with a reminder that we human beings are of animal origin—rational, yes, but possessed of all the characteristics of an animal: susceptible to scent, content to eat meat or masticate granola, instinctively equipped to engage in fisticuffs or flight, inclined to hibernate in November and marry in May. Indeed, whenever we ourselves wish to describe a nasty person we refer to him as a beast or—if clumsy—an ass. For example, in Charles Dickens's story "A Christmas Carol" Scrooge's nephew Fred initiates a charade in which his family must guess what animal he's thinking of. Gradually he's forced to admit it's a live animal, a disagreeable animal, an animal that growls and grunts, lives in London, doesn't live in a menagerie; nor is it a horse, a cow, a bull, or tiger. Finally Fred's plump sister-in-law cries out, "I know what it is, Fred! . . . It's your uncle Scro-o-o-o-ge!"[1]

Or consider that San Francisco writer, Frank Norris, who throughout his gripping story of life on Polk Street in the 1890s (titled *McTeague*) insinuates that human beings—beneath a veneer of civilization—still reflect their animal origins. For example, there's a description of one greedy character as having "thin . . . cat-like lips . . . eyes that had grown keen as those of a lynx . . . and clawlike, prehensile fingers."[2] He speaks of McTeague himself as possessing the qualities of a draught horse: "immensely strong, stupid, docile, obedient" or at other times behaving like a panther, lips drawn, fangs "aflash." Unable to think of what to call a man who insulted him, McTeague finally comes out with: "I'll thump you in the head, you little-you little-you little-little-little pup."

From page to page of his novel, Norris underscores his conviction that humanity has hardly begun to phase out of its primeval ferocity. In anticipation of a falling out between McTeague and his bosom buddy Marcus, Norris describes two fenced-in dogs trying to get at each other in a backyard: "Suddenly the quarrel had exploded on either side of the fence. . . . Their teeth gleamed. They tore at the fence with their front paws. They filled the whole night with their clamor." And Marcus cries out, "Just listen; wouldn't that make a fight if the two got together? Have to try it some day."

"Have to try it some day." How prophetic, because doesn't that backyard episode pretty much describe how the nations of the world (despite their civilized ways) have behaved toward each other over this past century—from the trench combat of the Great War to the current ferocity of the Middle East? No, it wasn't about harmony between literal wolves and lambs that Isaiah was dreaming when he spoke his prophecy, but about us, about a day when, under the influence of a radically new kind of humanity embodied in the Christ of Christmas, we might someday cease preying upon each other and begin praying and playing together as fully human beings.

SECOND SUNDAY OF ADVENT
OPTION

Matthew 3:1–12, Mark Twain

The Difference between Fantasy and Imagination

I'm a city boy who knows nothing about agriculture. I assume chaff is to a kernel of nutritious wheat what the husk is to an ear of golden corn—the outer wrapping. Fantasy is something like that. Fantasy may be called a cover-up to the true exercise of our imagination. Fantasy is what Hollywood dishes out to us every day: heroic action against formidable odds or romantic musicals in which the baritone is but the projection of myself in a final clinch with a soprano! Fantasy is wishful thinking, a shallow attempt to escape the monotony of the prosaic world of school, work, and domestic demands.

Tom Sawyer lived in such a fantasy world. "I ain't doing my duty by that boy," said his Aunt Polly. "He's full of the Old Scratch. . . . He'll play hooky this afternoon . . . he hates work more than he hates anything else."[3] What Tom preferred to do was take off for the woods or row out to an island in the river to create a world of his own. In that fantastic world Tom could become so many exciting things: a steamboat captain, a pirate, an Indian on the warpath. He could be Robin Hood, the lovable outlaw. Of course, all the dangers were custom-made to insure he experienced no pain. The cutlasses were make-believe and the slain cutthroat bounced quickly back to take another harmless shot at Tom's invulnerable hero. No smidgen of real fear or heroism was required.

That is, until one night Tom pushed the envelope too far. He and Huck Finn had decided to test the theory that you could cure a wart by going to a cemetery after midnight and throwing a dead cat at the devil when he came to carry off the soul of a recently buried sinner. But once there, they witnessed from behind a tombstone an argument among actual grave robbers during which one (Muff Potter) was knocked unconscious and another slain by a mean third party named Joe. Suddenly a heavy dose of reality had intruded on Tom's fantasy world. Did Tom tackle the challenge heroically? Not by a long sight. He and Huck hightailed it back to the now cherished safety of that ordinary world they both despised and kept a low profile for weeks!

It was only after Tom learned that Joe had blamed Muff Potter for the murder and that Muff was to be tried (and probably hanged) that something began to grow within Tom's soul. Call it shame, call it compassion, call it true courage or a blend of all three. I'd call it his creative as opposed to his escapist imagination. In other words, the kernel, the seedling of true heroism, had begun to emerge at long last from within the mere chaff of his fantasy world.

Well, you know what happened. Tom overcame his fear of Joe. He showed up as the surprise witness at Muff's trial and by telling the truth saved Muff's life. He did something heroic, self-sacrificial, something really imaginative instead of merely imaginary. He performed a virtuous deed—something bound to make him a legend after all—capable of nurturing the imaginations of other boys and girls for ages to come.

Where do we stand in relation to fantasy and imagination? Do we dream our lives away in scenarios that allow us to upstage everyone? Or are we ready to emancipate our imaginations from such sterile use and apply it to the wants, the pain, the injustices of the real world around us—creatively, virtuously, beautifully? John the Baptist tells us Christ is coming soon and with Christ a formidable Spirit or Wind whose aim will be to blow away the chaff of mere fantasy in our lives—and by doing so release that kernel of a more nutritious imagination to follow Christ courageously wherever he may lead us.

THIRD SUNDAY OF ADVENT

Matthew 11:2–11, Allen Ginsberg, William Wordsworth

Coming to Our Senses

God seems to have been more present to people in ancient times. Read the older stories of the Bible and you find Adam, Noah, and Abraham in familiar conversation with their Maker. Angels appear with great frequency, delivering directions and warnings. God appears in a burning tree to Moses and as a vocal cloud on Mount Sinai. For that matter, the literature of the pagan world is also full of supernatural appearances, as are all those stories read to us as children that begin with "Once upon a time." This raises a question: How come we don't see angels and elves or hear God's voice resounding in any startling way nowadays? What's happened to the magic?

Well, we've "matured" beyond all need for God and an accentuated sense of things spiritual. We have become masters of our own fate in a purely secular world. We use our heads and discredit our imaginations. We are convinced that nature is simply exploitable matter to be investigated by science and mastered by technology to serve our material well-being. Our probes into outer space reveal no "heaven" there. For all we know, we are alone in this vast universe and that's that. Close up the Bible—indeed, box up all nursery tales as well and store them in a closet. They're not relevant any more.

And yet we are not happy over this so-called enlightenment. We don't like being alone in the universe no matter how much our stoical experts tell us to accept the "fact." Our malaise is evident in the popularity of all the science fiction we see on TV—about people like Captain Picard who weekly seek out new worlds, new civilizations. Why? Because, godless though we may be, we still desperately want to find someone else to talk to besides ourselves.

This malaise over the eviction of the spiritual from our world is also evident in the desperate behavior and literature of the late twentieth-century Hip generation whose poet Allen Ginsberg in his lamentation called "Howl" wrote:

> I saw the best minds of my generation destroyed by madness,
>> starving hysterical naked,
> dragging themselves through . . . streets at dawn looking for
>> an angry fix,
> angelheaded hipsters burning for the ancient heavenly
>> connection
>>> to the starry dynamo in the machinery of night . . . [4]

The same malaise was evident as far back as the poet Wordsworth, who, looking at the sea one day and feeling nothing, cried out:

> It moves us not—Great God! I'd rather be
> A Pagan suckled in a creed outworn;
> So might I, standing on this pleasant lea,
> Have glimpses that would make me less forlorn
> Have sight of Proteus rising from the sea;
> Or hear old Triton blow his wreathed horn.[5]

As Advent comes around may we not as modern Christians join in this chorus of complaint? Once upon a time this season of prolonged and chilly nights was made bearable by the faint carols of approaching angels, but even that signal of God's reality has been lost amid the din of seasonal commerce and hollow ballads about chestnuts, snow, jingle bells, and red-nosed reindeers—about everything but the Christ for whom Christmas is named.

This is why, of course, we come crowding to church today— to revive our spiritual sense of things, to hear Isaiah promise us that this parched desert we have made of our world can blossom again, become musical again with the presence of God. And we come to

hear John the Baptist once more ask Christ, on our behalf, from the
depths of his prison and ours: are you the one who is to come—to
bring light and poetry back into our lives and behavior? To which
Christ will respond (in so many words): "If you've been made blind,
deaf, lame, and well-nigh lifeless by the secular atmosphere you
breathe today, I am and ever will be your key to a fresh way of seeing,
hearing, and dancing your way through a world become a Christmas
Story again!"

FOURTH SUNDAY OF ADVENT

Matthew 1:18–24

The Nativity: A Time to Consult the Ledger

The New Testament evangelists offer us not only beautiful descriptions of the birth of Jesus but a contrast to ponder. *On the one hand,*
we have King Herod who feigns interest in the arrival of Jesus but
actually feels threatened by the news and immediately conspires to
erase Jesus as disruptive of the status quo—even if it takes overkill:
the massacre of every infant born in Bethlehem.

Then there's Zachary. He's certainly not a ruthless man like
Herod, but he is cautious. The news that his aged wife is pregnant
with John the Baptist as prelude to a radical change within Judaism
makes him balk instead of rejoice. After a long career as a priest at
the Temple, Zachary is not enthusiastic about novelty. All his life he
has kept to a routine, presiding over a predictable cycle of sacrificial
services guided by rubrics designed to standardize his every gesture
and word—relieving him of any necessity to think. And he has
come to enjoy being a maintenance man, a cog within a smooth
running machine. Ever preferring a low profile to any kind of
troublesome notoriety, he is now shaken by the sudden attention
of an angel who, regardless of the rubrics, interrupts Zachary's

service and invites him to become involved in events of cosmic impact. "Pardon me," says Zachary, "I'd rather not." The consequence? The angel says, "All right, you prefer a quiet life to one of adventure? Then quiet—mute—you shall remain. Your potential for an eloquent existence will remain bottled up within you until at times you will feel like you are about to burst!"

And then, of course, there's Joseph in today's Gospel reading, whose hesitancy to be involved in something marvelous is due more to his sense of propriety. To engage a girl who is already pregnant is simply asking for trouble. The prudent thing to do is to disengage and return to his prior and tranquil anonymity.

So there you have one side of the ledger (Herod, Zachary, and Joseph) to remind us of our own tendency to retain absolute control over whatever happens within of our petty domain; to cling to a comfortable routine; to "appear" proper rather than risk participating in a drama, a tragicomedy bigger than ourselves.

On the other hand, the Gospel writers present us with the Magi who are not at all reluctant to follow a star across miles of desert in expectation of some grand discovery—to risk their lives and invest their treasure in something that seems pregnant with good for the whole of humanity. And then there's Joseph, again in today's Gospel, who lets his dreams overrule his prudence to make his a name to be remembered down through all generations.

And, of course, there's Mary, the truly pivotal character of the whole account. In contrast to Zachary she is simply an affirmative soul: "Be it done to me according to your word." Though it promises to break her heart, she's quite ready to let God's Spirit infiltrate her very being to make of her a means whereby the world will be turned upside down, where grace will have begun to overrule our instinct for mere survival.

Confronted by these different responses to invitations to come out of our precious privacy, to go that extra mile and save a world, on which side of the ledger do we see ourselves? Frankly, while I don't think I've ever been as paranoid as King Herod,

Zachary fits me to a T. But then it's never too late, for eventually Zachary did begin to believe in miracles and not only recovered his voice but found out he could even sing!

THE NATIVITY OF THE LORD, MASS AT MIDNIGHT

Luke 2:1–14, W. H. Auden

Oratorio

Back in 1941 W. H. Auden composed a Christmas oratorio entitled "For The Time Being"[6] in which, pivoting around tonight's Gospel, he offers us a poetic paraphrase of the whole Christmas story. He begins by suggesting the similarity of the world when Jesus was born with the way things are today. Then as now, he says, the secular world had gone cold. With little academic hope of immortality, time had become meaningless, each day a drag. And even if people retained a notion they might count for something in the cosmic scheme of things, they were encouraged to get over such illusions. They might as well resign themselves to being digits in the benign hands of society's demographers.

> Darkness and snow descend;
> The clock on the mantelpiece
> Has nothing to recommend,
> Nor does the face in the glass
> Appear nobler than our own
> As darkness and snow descend
> On all personality.

> Yet in the hearts of people an overwhelming persuasion
lingered

. . . that somewhere, over the high hill,
Under the roots of the oak, in the depths of the sea,
Is a womb . . .

out of which a more resplendent awareness of world and self might emerge. And sure enough, in response to that lingering persuasion or plea, the angel Gabriel appears to Mary:

Hear, child, what I am sent to tell:
Love wills your dream to happen, so
Love's will on earth may be, through you
No longer a pretend but true.

Even as the angel alerts Mary to something wonderful about to happen, by Christmas a whole chorus of angels appears to the shepherds to proclaim:

Unto you a Child,
A Son is given,
Praising, proclaiming
The ingression of Love,
Earth's darkness invents
The blaze of Heaven,
And frigid silence
Meditates a song.

To which our shepherds reply:

Tonight for the first time the prison gates
Have opened. . . .
Music and sudden light . . .
Have interrupted our routine . . .
And swept the filth of habit from our hearts . . .
O here and now our endless journey starts.

And now a star entices the Magi (in Auden's mind they are scientist, abstract philosopher, and moralizer) to make that scary journey beyond their rigid principles and each responds:

> To discover how to be truthful now
> . . . how to be living now
> . . . how to be loving now
> Is the reason I follow this star.

And soon around the crèche they assemble with the shepherds to sing in unison:

> Released by Love from isolating wrong,
> Let us for Love unite our various song,
> Each with his gift according to his kind
> Bringing this child his body and his mind.

Still there was old King Herod to deal with—symbol of systems that refuse to make any leap of faith. There he sits in his castle content that the trains are running on time, barges are unloading fertilizer at the river wharves, soft drinks and sandwiches may be had a reasonable price, highways are in good repair, and no counterfeit coins have been found of late. There he sits content that everything is so rationally arranged, yet disturbed over this obstinate need his citizens have for something supernatural—despite his legislation forbidding anyone over the age of 12 to believe in fairies, despite fines he has imposed on Ouija boards and playing cards and all such symptoms of hope!

And then along comes this trio from the East with an ecstatic grin on their scholarly faces, telling him God has been born! It really must be stopped or else

> Reason will be replaced by Revelation . . . .
> Justice will be replaced by Pity as the cardinal human
>   virtue, and

all fear of retribution will vanish. Every cornerboy
> will congratulate
himself: "I'm such a sinner that God had to come down
> in person to
save me. I must be a devil of a fellow." . . .

Naturally this cannot be allowed to happen. Civilization
must be saved even if this means sending for the military. . . .

> . . . O dear, Why couldn't this infant be born somewhere else?
> Why can't people be sensible? I don't want to be horrid.

And so shortly after every Christmas Jesus, Mary, and
Joseph must flee to Egypt while for the time being (until another
Christmas comes along) we are left

> Remembering the stable where for once in our lives
> Everything became a You and nothing was an It.

THE HOLY FAMILY OF JESUS, MARY, AND JOSEPH

Matthew 2:13–15, 19–23

Una Meditazione Caravaggesca

The Gospel account of the flight of Jesus, Mary, and Joseph into
Egypt is very sparse on detail, too sparse to satisfy the imagination
of later generations. Consequently, Christian storytellers began to
work into the account miraculous items befitting so sacred a
journey. Date trees bend down to relieve the Holy Family's hunger.
Angels appear to help them cross broad rivers. Fields of wheat
sprout up along their path in the desert. Egyptian idols go toppling
off their pedestals. What started out as a flight from Herod
becomes—in subsequent legend—an extraordinary excursion

of the infant Christ into the Gentile world well in advance of his
later missionaries.

The great Italian artist Caravaggio, who introduced an
astonishing realism in the art of the seventeenth century, was a
beneficiary of such legendary detail and used it in his 1599 depiction
of the journey. His painting dwells on the Holy Family's pausing to
rest en route to Egypt. He divides the scene in two. On the left we
see an aged Joseph, his long, gray hair and beard uncombed, his face
in shadow. He's clearly worn out. Below the hem of his somber
brown garb we see him rubbing one sore foot on the other. On the
ground beside him lies everything he owns wrapped up in a pillow
case plus a basket-entwined bottle corked with a wad of paper.
Behind him we see the deeper brown hide of an ass, ears pointed
back and one limpid eye peering over Joseph's shoulder. Darkness,
weariness, and old age weigh heavily on this side of the picture,
along with a barrenness accentuated by several sharp stones that
litter the ground near Joseph's feet.

How different that is from the right side of the painting
where our focus falls on Mary and the infant Christ. Here we
behold color, light, fertility, nourishment, a tree-lined river, and
a blue dawn revealing the only landscape Caravaggio ever painted.
The rocks on Joseph's side of the picture give way on Mary's side
to the foliage of plants, grass, and even strands of wheat. And Mary
and her cherubic child, both sound asleep, are bathed in a light
made even brighter by Mary's wine-red gown.

It's as though Caravaggio wanted to picture the contrast
between the Old and New Testaments, between a world not yet
illuminated by Christ and one alive with his presence and Gospel.
On the left there is darkness, weariness, an unsettled and footsore
Joseph, symbolic of frequently exiled Israel; on the right there is
a promising blue horizon, living water, the tree of life, eucharistic
wheat, and Mary as Mother Church, cradling the light of the world.

But that's not all! The painting is divided by the presence of
a central figure: an adolescent angel playing a violin. He stands with

his back to us, his body partly wrapped in a garment as white and windblown as a cloud. He directs his playing toward Joseph, who, like a human music stand, holds up the angel's sheet music which contains a 1519 Flemish composition based on a verse from the Song of Songs: "How beautiful you are, how pleasing, my love, my delight." The verse, of course, is applied to Mary and quite appropriately, for Caravaggio's Mary is indeed a delight to behold. The angel certainly must think so, because he's been playing with such intensity he's broken one of his violin strings.

But going back to the left and right halves of Caravaggio's painting, do I not find the contrast applicable to myself? Or perhaps I should say the "transition" I'm ever in the middle of? On the one hand, I feel like Joseph, weary, running away from things, footsore, heartsore, wanting simply to sit down and never budge an inch. And yet, stimulated by the angelic music of God's Word, am I not ever seduced by the Church to pass over into that verdant terrain of Jesus and Mary where my soul may begin to blossom, where I may share the dreams they dream and sense the dawn they sense is rising? It's never too late to make that transition. After all, in the painting Joseph looks as old as I do—and he made it!

EPIPHANY

Matthew 2:1–12, Anne Porter

The Ticket

Has it ever occurred to you that neither Herod nor his scribes could see the star the Magi saw? Otherwise they might have followed it themselves to discover the place where Jesus lay. No, only the Magi could see the star and that was because they were visionaries, men who believed in the possibility of the impossible.

Men like Herod and his scribes had no such inclination. Having a somewhat paranoid view of reality, they feared the possible as much as the impossible. Their minds were closed to any other notion of reality than the self-justifying one they possessed and, therefore, so were their hearts, their imaginations, their eyes. They saw no star. What's more, in their later massacre of the innocents they reveal their determination to prevent others from seeing any stars, any deeper meaning to life. They reveal their determination to eradicate all visionaries and poets, to repress the creative imagination every child is born with—all notion, for instance, that life for each of us could be in any way a journey of the Magi whereby we feel we too are following some star toward realms and experiences ineffable.

For instance, Herod might have scoffed at me when as a boy of 14 I was accepted by a seminary situated on New York's Hudson River, a mind-boggling 130 miles from my home in Philadelphia and, as I read the train schedule, became fascinated by the names of the stations along the way: Tarrytown, Ossining, Croton-on-Hudson, Verplanck, Peekskill, Garrison. "It's nothing but a train schedule," Herod might say. But to me each name was exotic. Each stimulated my imagination the way the names of towns and people in some novel seduce one into reading on to discover what might happen beyond the novel's opening page. This was to be for me no mere journey from one place to another (as Herod might declare) but a journey of discovery at the end of which I might eventually find my Self—even as the Magi found an infant in a manger.

Be like the Magi. Be like the poets among us. Never lose confidence in your imagination, in your conviction that life is more profound than the media and business world and habit make it out to be. Never lose sight of the star, the sparkle you sense you see in the people around you and the seemingly insignificant things you experience in life. Be like the Catholic poet Anne Porter who one day found a ticket in her purse and had no idea what it was for. It had a number on it and the words INDIANA TICKET COMPANY.

On the reverse side it said KEEP THIS TICKET. And so she did—
on the night table beside her bed—because being a poet she knew
it to be no mere stub of paper but a signal of dimensions exciting—
or as she puts it:

> I keep it carefully
> Because I'm old
> Which means
> I'll soon be leaving
> For another country
>
> Where possibly
> Some blinding-bright
> Enormous angel
> Will stop me
> At the border
>
> And ask
> To see my ticket.[7]

THE BAPTISM OF THE LORD

Matthew 3:13–17, Daniel Defoe, John Milton

Out of the Depths I Cry to Thee; Lord, Hear My Voice

"The wave that came upon me again buried me at once twenty or
thirty feet deep in its own body; and I could feel myself carried with
a mighty force and swiftness towards the shore . . . I was ready
to burst with holding my breath, when, as I felt myself rising up,
so, to my immediate relief, I found my head and hands shoot out
above the surface of the water. . . . I struck forward against the
return of the waves and felt ground with my feet. I stood still a few

moments . . . and then took to my heels . . . towards the shore. But neither would this deliver me from the fury of the sea, which came pouring after me again; and . . . dashed me against a piece of a rock, and that with such force, that it left me senseless . . . and had it returned again immediately, I must have been strangled in the water."[8]

Thus does Daniel Defoe describe Robinson Crusoe's eventual escape from the clutches of an ocean that consumed all of his shipmates. How often have similar stories been told, with some surviving the ordeal and many never retrieved? The same scene is played out in Melville's *Moby Dick* and Shakespeare's *The Tempest* and Milton's famous lament, "Lycidas," over a college friend who drowned in the Irish Sea. The tradition goes all the way back to the biblical Jonah, who, having been tossed overboard in a storm, remembers how "the flood enveloped me . . . breakers and billows passed over me. . . . The waters swirled about me . . . seaweed clung about my head. Down I went to the roots of the mountains" (Jonah 2:4–7).

I suppose such stories fascinate us because they aptly portray (metaphorically) our own situation. How often do we describe ourselves as deluged with bills or work; washed up; caught in the undertow of a friend's addiction? Sometimes, day after day, it seems like we're constantly having to come up for air lest we be dragged down not just by the ordinary demands of life but by all those more ominous denizens that dwell beneath the shadow of our smile: things like resentment, envy, sloth, vindictiveness, greed, doubt, despair.

Perhaps it's because we all do at times experience a "sinking feeling" that the Bible often chooses to describe our ultimate redemption in terms of a rescue from deep water. Think about it. God doesn't leave Jonah submerged but deposits him on dry land to commence his life anew. Nor does God allow the infant Moses to perish in the waters of the Nile but rescues him to lead his whole nation out of the Red Sea. Nor does God allow Noah to drown in a sea of troubles, nor Joshua and his people to be swept away by the current of the Jordan River, but insists that the river part to allow

Israel to walk dry shod into the Promised Land. Nor, at the very beginning of Genesis, does God allow the primeval deep to prevail but, having breathed over it, cries out: "Let the dry land appear", thereby giving humanity a foothold whence it might evolve.

Today's Gospel reading offers us a climactic sequel to all those other biblical episodes of marine rescue, for in it we behold Jesus (like a new Moses or Joshua) rising out of the depths that would drag us down—waters that symbolize ignorance, depression, and meanness—yes, our very mortality that would suffocate us, but from which Christ and his Gospel have the power to deliver us and send us on our way—hopeful and thereby as dynamically creative as Christ himself.

Such was the Christian faith John Milton expressed when he consoled himself over the drowning death of his young friend in those forever memorable words:

> Weep no more . . .
> For Lycidas, your sorrow, is not dead,
> Sunk though he be beneath the wat'ry floor;
> So sinks the day-star in the ocean bed,
> And yet anon repairs his drooping head,
> And tricks his beams, and with new-spangled ore
> Flames in the forehead of the morning sky:
> So Lycidas sunk low, but mounted high,
> Through the dear might of him that walked the waves.[9]

~~~~~~~~~~~~~~~~~~~~~~~~~~~~~~

FIRST SUNDAY OF LENT

Matthew 4:1–11, Melissa Kay

Lenten Prelude

I have on my desk a photograph of my son Philip with one of his friends, both about 22 years old. It was taken near Clay and Kearny Streets in San Francisco outside the cheap hotel where they rented rooms. Philip is wearing his usual raincoat to hide a body he never liked, he is bearded to hide a face he never liked, and he's probably high on something to forget a world he never liked. His friend, the survivor of two suicide attempts and disowned by his psychiatrist father, is also heavily bearded. Each has an affectionate arm around the other's shoulder as they pose against a background of Chinese restaurants—and each will be dead within months of each other shortly after this photo was taken.

When Philip was born I never anticipated he would become involved with drugs, which would ravage his body, damage an eye, and insure his early demise. Like many a well-educated, employable middle-class parent I assumed our family life would be jolly, like that of those *Leave It To Beaver* comedies. In other words, I was naive enough to imagine my life would be without problems, certainly without anguish. And I anticipated perennially sending out one of those standard Christmas letters to friends, brimming with good news and proud descriptions of my children's many achievements. Little did I realize that Philip's arrival would put an end to all such self-indulgent illusions, that he would awaken me to the fact that no domestic situation is immune to pain.

Pain, of course, is something that we who live under the dominion of Pollyanna like to deny. Indeed, as a nation, in our pursuit of an anesthetized happiness, we have marshaled all our technology to thwart pain by way of dreamboats or preemptive strikes or pills or the daily news, whose display of other people's pain makes us feel exempt.

But pain and anguish are an inevitable part of life and after my experience with Phil I have come to believe anguish to be a sacrament—because sacraments are vehicles of God's grace, and ever since Philip's brief sojourn among us I find myself on the other side of a divide—as though I had crossed a Red Sea and wandered through a wilderness only to arrive at a more tender state of mind than I possessed when I dwelled among the fleshpots of Egypt. It's a state of mind or soul that can be best defined as vulnerable and, if vulnerable, then potentially compassionate, and—if potentially compassionate—can one be far from the state of mind possessed by Christ, who, rejecting the comfortable alternatives offered him by Satan in today's Gospel, chose to identify with the anguished of this world (which, if we are honest, means with all of us) and thereby revealed God's might to reside in nothing less than his absolutely compassionate love.

But this is so much prose. Perhaps it is better said by way of a poem written by Phil's mother shortly after his death titled "A Hymn To My Son." It goes like this:

> Perhaps dark, rough people need Angels of Light—
> To soften them, untangle their hair, bring calm to their hands.
> But we were already light, and bright, pressed and correct—
> We needed—if to break open our courteous hearts—
> An Unwashed Angel—uncombed and unshaven—grace
> Streaming from the cry of electric strings,
> Reaching out, shaking us in the night
> From our too moderate dreams,
> As he, single-eyed, lifting into his heart
> Park dwellers, street saints, the hermits of the hotels,
> Cried out, "See! See! These are my friends!"
> Until we cracked open our eyes and, holding his sooted hands,
> Followed him, weeping, into the Sorrow of God.[10]

SECOND SUNDAY OF LENT

Genesis 12:1–4, Nathaniel Hawthorne

All the King's Horses and All the King's Men

Conversion is rarely a sudden thing. It often plays itself out over time. For example, today we read of Abraham's first call to follow God out of familiar surroundings "to a land that I will show you." The invitation was vague but, to his credit, Abraham moved out— until he reached God's destination and saw people dying of starvation all around him, for "there was a famine in the land." Immediately Abraham's old reflexes kicked in and he hightailed it back to his old environment, until God propelled him out again. And that's the way it went: two steps forward, one step back; three steps forward, two steps back—until he arrived at that prolific state of confidence and peace that won him the title "Father of all believers."

Saint Peter's conversion was just as gradual. Despite the Gospel's saying he immediately left his nets and followed Jesus, Peter remained for a long time entangled in his old ways. He was the kind of fellow who, when he experiences a new insight, tries hard to fit it into his habitual frame of reference. In Peter's mind his nation was God's elect and all others were profane. Redemption meant the victory of a theocratic Israel. And so for a long time Peter tried to interpret Jesus in these terms. He tried to pour the fascinating wine of Jesus into old wineskins. He was especially shocked when Jesus predicted his trial and execution and, when it happened, he denied any association with the victim. He remained trapped in the clarity of his old mind-set in which victory meant victory and defeat meant head for the hills and the devil take the hindmost!

Of course, the Resurrection and Pentecost snapped him out of it again. Under these extraordinary experiences, he opened his mind to a fresher understanding of what Jesus was all about (namely, grace, love, and peace). He even began to stand in Jesus' place before the Temple hierarchy of his day—he, a workingman without credentials, explaining things to authorities who used explain things to him! Still he remained entangled in past habits of mind. He clung to old notions of what was unclean: certain kinds of animals and all Romans as well—so that God had to shout, "You are not to call unclean what God considers clean." And then God propelled him into the house of a Roman, where he found God's Spirit quite as likely to be present as in any Hebrew household. Again, two steps backward, three steps forward!

Peter's progress remained gradual even after that. The last we read of him in Antioch, Saint Paul is confronting him about his persistent inclination to sit only at table with Jewish—not Gentile—Christians. But should we condemn Peter for the hesitancies of his conversion process? How can we, since his story is but a mirror of our own hesitant approach to wholesomeness of vision and behavior?

In this we, along with Peter, are like old Hepzibah Pyncheon in Hawthorne's *The House of the Seven Gables*. She lived entangled in aristocratic illusions of herself. She looked with disdain on the world around her, until grace in the form of poverty forced her to open a "cent shop," to open her closed mansion to experiences that would put her in contact with God's wider world and release her truer self. She didn't like it. It involved her in little frustrations, as when (while arranging her window display) she spilled a whole box of marbles all over the floor, forcing her to get down on her knees to gather them up. Yet what a marvelous symbol of how God often has to scatter or shatter our old way of seeing things, if only in the end to bring us to our knees, to reintegrate our lives around something bigger and deeper than our tired old habits of pride and prejudice.

THIRD SUNDAY OF LENT

John 4:5–42, Seamus Heaney

Truth Lies at the Bottom of a Deep Well (An Old Saying)

"As a child, they could not keep me from wells."[11] So begins a poem by the Irish poet Seamus Heaney.

> I loved the dark drop, the trapped sky . . .
>
> I savored the rich crash when a bucket
> Plummeted down at the end of a rope.
> So deep you saw no reflection in it.

Wells have fascinated human beings from as far back as we can remember, probably because there's something mysterious about a deep, dark shaft that reaches down to hidden waters—as though it were a corridor to the very source of the universe. Hence the popular belief in wishing wells. There's one old well near the river Tyne in England out of which archeologists have retrieved close to 13,500 coins dating from between 41 and 383 AD—no doubt tossed into the well to obtain a favor from some pre-Christian deity.

But Christians themselves were hardly to be outdone in this regard. There are sacred wells all over Europe to which pilgrims travel to this very day to seek beneficial contact with not just the bottom of a well but with the Foundation and Wellspring of all creation, God. In Kildare there's Saint Bridget's Well, and in Wales there's Saint David's Well and the famous Well of Saint Winifred dating back some 1,200 years.

And think how often wells are featured in the Bible! For instance, there's the story of Sarah's maid Hagar and her infant son Ishmael, who were left alone to die in the desert, when along came an angel to point out a well that saved their lives. And then there's

Jacob's Well beside which Jesus conversed with that Samaritan woman. Jacob's Well was more than a source of water to the Samaritans. Reaching down into it, they were reaching not only for water but symbolically reaching down through time itself to Jacob and the God of Jacob, the wellspring of their religious heritage. The Gospel of John also mentions the healing pool of Bethesda and the pool of Siloam to which Jesus sent a blind man to wash and regain his sight.

Of course, we live in a secular age that smiles at belief in wishing wells. But are wishing wells really out of date? What are all the sciences and humanities taught at our secular universities but wishing wells of a sort? Aren't geologists and philosophers and biologists and geneticists and anthropologists and paleontologists and psychologists all peering into matter and back through time, seeking the origin, the meaning of life and this universe, looking for some wellspring? And what's a telescope but a kind of well down which astronomers gaze at our starry past to relieve our ignorance about what we are if not who we are? Or take literature and poetry. What are they but attempts to plumb the mysteries of nature and human existence? Seamus Heaney admits he has become too old to go bending Narcissus-like over literal wells. It's beneath his adult dignity. Instead, he says:

> I rhyme
> To see myself, to set the darkness echoing.

As for me, I'm not that modern or secular that I would forgo a chance to visit one of those pilgrimage wells like Saint Winifred's to make a wish. I'm still Catholic enough to think sacramentally and see in all things great and small some glimmer of the spiritual origin of our world. And wells must especially have that quality, considering that Jesus chose one day to say of himself: "Let anyone who thirsts come to me and drink," thereby describing himself as a wellspring out of which all humanity might experience the true meaning of life. And then he went on to say, "Whoever believes in me, as scripture says: 'Rivers of living water will flow from within him.'" And what does that mean but that, my thirst relieved by Christ, I may myself become a wishing well, a source of profound spiritual refreshment to all who come in contact with me?

FOURTH SUNDAY OF LENT

John 9:1–41, E. M. Forster

A Room with a View

"The Signora had no business to do it," complained Charlotte Bartlett in E. M. Forster's 1908 novel *A Room With a View.*[12] "She promised us south rooms with a view . . . instead of which here are north rooms, looking into a courtyard." Miss Bartlett had good reason to be upset. As chaperone to her cousin, Lucy Honeychurch, it was her job to ensure that Lucy's first trip to Italy and her current sojourn in Florence would be a pleasant change from foggy old England. And yet here they were, assigned to lodging that looked out not upon a panorama of Florence's domes and towers and ancient bridges but upon a backyard.

Miss Bartlett's complaint was overheard by Mr. Emerson, an old fellow who shared their breakfast table. "I have a view," he said brusquely. "This is my son . . . . He has a view, too. . . . What I mean is that you can have our rooms. . . . We'll change." Well, much as she disliked their assigned rooms, Miss Bartlett had no wish to be under obligation to total strangers. Her British propriety required that she refuse the offer, which she took to be a rude invasion of her privacy. "Thank you very much indeed; that is out of the question," she replied. Mr. Emerson was not the type to give in so easily. Placing his fists on the table, he asked, "Why?"—which only made Miss Bartlett redden with displeasure.

Well, did she or did she not want a room with a view? Having traveled so far did she or did she not want to experience Italy? Her very choice of a place to stay in Florence makes you wonder. The Pension Bertolini was a thoroughly British "island" in the midst of Florence. All the guests were genteel English ladies and proper British gentlemen. The so-called "signorina" who managed the place had a Cockney accent straight out of London. The dining room was graced with a portrait of Queen Victoria and a schedule of services at the local Anglican Church—all of which compelled Lucy to remark, "Charlotte, don't you feel . . . we might be in London? I can hardly believe that all kinds of other things are just outside."

But before we condemn Miss Bartlett's obvious ambivalence about truly experiencing Italy, truly leaving Britain behind, let's consider our own ambivalence when it comes to Christ's offering us by way of his Gospel "a room with a view." We live such enclosed lives. We long to escape this enclosure, the confinement of our pettiness, our egocentric concerns, worries, and biases for a fresher view of reality. And along comes Christ with a Gospel that can open us up the way a view of Florence in all of its splendor might. And yet as individuals and a Church we hesitate. We cling to familiar ways; we rationalize ourselves into remaining stuck right where we are. Like Miss Bartlett, we close the shutters upon a view and a way of being too blindingly bright, too potentially wonderful (and demanding) to be tolerable.

Not so with Lucy. When at last Miss Bartlett gave in to the Emersons and accepted their "rooms with a view," while Miss Bartlett spent her first moments investigating her room's interior to make sure all shutters and doors had locks, Lucy, yielding to her inner need to be free of "Britain" and "propriety" and "security," flung wide the windows to her room and leaned out into the sunshine to take in the beautiful hills, the marble churches, the gurgling Arno, the crowded trams and somersaulting children, the band and comic opera soldiers, and the white bullocks coming out of an archway—life, world, people in all their wonder and worth, releasing Lucy's repressed capacity for universal love!

Is there a shuttered window within our psyches behind which, like Miss Bartlett, we repress our yearning for light and beauty, insulate ourselves from all surprise? We must let Christ open those shutters, touch our eyes—our souls—as he did Miss Lucy's (whose name implies light) and that of the young man in today's Gospel. To put it in an even more profoundly Lenten way: we must let him and his angels roll away the stone behind which we have lain buried for far too long.

FIFTH SUNDAY OF LENT

John 11:1–45, William Butler Yeats

Lazarus

In a brief play called *Calvary*[13] by William Butler Yeats, Lazarus appears amid the crowd watching Jesus carry his cross up that tragic hill. The people press forward

> To shout their mockery: 'Work a miracle,'
> Cries one, 'and save your self'; another cries,
> 'Call on your father now before your bones
> Have been picked bare by the great desert birds';

Jesus notices Lazarus in the crowd and says:

> Seeing that you died,
> Lay in the tomb four days and were raised up,
> You will not mock at me.

But Lazarus does indeed harbor resentment toward Jesus:

> For four whole days
> I had been dead and I was lying still
> In an old comfortable mountain cavern
> When you came climbing there with a great crowd
> And dragged me to the light.

Christ responds:

> I called your name . . .
> I gave you life.

But Lazarus feels no gratitude:

> 'Come out!' you called;
> You dragged me to the light as boys drag out
> A rabbit when they have dug its hole away;
> And now with all the shouting at your heels
> You travel towards the death I am denied.

Lazarus did not want to be raised from the dead. Life was too much for him. He longed for a place to hide. But Jesus—with his insistence that we live, that we cross every threshold we encounter, that we grieve and grow—flooded with light that deathly solitude, that corner where Lazarus thought he might lie safe forever.

This is indeed what Jesus came to do. He came to contradict our inclination to withdraw from people, from pain and effort, from our potential for mistakes—to avoid any revelations that might shatter our complacency. And so he shouts again and again: "Lazarus, William, Mary, Margaret—come forth! Do not resist gestation, do not abort your own becoming." For it is this reluctance to BE that would drag our universe back into the darkness out of which God called it in Genesis. It is this reluctance to BE, to grow, to go through the never-ending agony of blossoming that generates so much of the negativity we read about everyday, that generates even the hope of the fundamentalist that doomsday may be imminent, that our untidy world might soon come to an end so that we might remain unchangeable for all eternity (which is a pious way of wishing to be dead).

Jesus would reverse such depression and the meanness it often generates. He summons us to life, hope, humor, compassion, love, solidarity—things that make a cynic's skin crawl. Like the Lazarus of Yeats's play we may—in our moodier moments—resist his summons. We may hope the stone behind which we would forever hide will stay put, block all resonance of his call to come out and grow.

But to no avail. The womb, our self-appointed tomb, cannot be our final resting place. His wake-up call will ultimately be too commanding, too challenging to resist, and we will stagger (reluctantly perhaps) out of our timidity before life (with all its variables) to hear his next even more frightening yet seductive command: "Untie him, unbind her; let them go free—to become the saints, the poets, the perennial beauties God intends them to be."

PALM SUNDAY OF THE LORD'S PASSION

Matthew 26:14—27:66 (specifically 26:69–75), Flannery O'Connor

And Immediately a Cock Crowed. Then Peter Remembered . . .

As if my inferiority complex were not severe enough, I now have to put up with those gorgeously arrogant roosters who condescend to share the Sonoma Plaza with me every morning. But my resentment soon gives way when, upon hearing them crow at sunrise, I remember it was just such a sound that awoke Peter to his cowardice and hypocrisy and turned him into a genuine saint. And I think: could that cock-a-doodle-doo Peter heard have been meant for me as well and does it now echo out of these Plaza descendants of that proud rooster of long ago?

We all need a wake-up call now and then as did Mrs. Turpin in Flannery O'Connor's story "Revelation."[14] Mrs. Turpin lived in the South of the 1950s. As the story begins we find her in a small town doctor's waiting room. Seated around the space are a well-dressed, pleasant looking woman and her stout 19-year-old college daughter who's reading a book and, by contrast, an old woman in tennis shoes, a sniveling child in a dirty romper, and its "white-trashy" mother wearing bedroom slippers.

The scene makes Mrs. Turpin recall a frequent daydream of hers in which she ponders the various levels of Southern society. At the bottom are the "colored" people, then come the "white-trash," then people who own a house, then people (like her) who own a house and land—and so on up the ladder. As usual the daydream leaves her feeling how blessed she is to be so middle class, superior to those below her. Soon she's engaged in conversation with the nice lady, addressing matters like the poor work ethic of black employees. Occasionally both have to put up with "crude" comments of the "white-trashy" woman. Possibly disturbed by the odor of the woman's child, Mrs. Turpin remarks that she raises hogs that are "cleaner than some children I've seen."

All the while Mrs. Turpin notices that the nice lady's college daughter keeps staring at her with increasing hostility over the edge of her book. It makes Mrs. Turpin uncomfortable but nothing happens until Mrs. Turpin exclaims in a fit of self-satisfaction: "When I think who all I could have been besides myself and what all I got, a little of everything, and a good disposition besides, I just feel like shouting, 'Thank you, Jesus, for making everything the way it is!'" At this point the college girl's book hits Mrs. Turpin right over her left eye and a tussle ensues and concludes with the college girl's whispering, "Go back to hell where you came from, you old wart hog!"

Now there's a wake-up call! Sometimes God has to resort to a little shock to snap us out of a deadly complacency that's become a way of life. The blow certainly had that effect on Mrs. Turpin. At home she fretted over the experience. She couldn't believe anyone

would think her an old wart hog, in any way mean or insensitive.
But as she hosed down the hogs that evening, her mind was now
vacant enough to see the purple streak in the evening sky turn into
"a vast, swinging bridge extending upward from the earth through
a field of living fire."

On it was a horde of souls ascending to heaven, white trash,
bands of black people in white robes, "battalions of freaks and luna-
tics shouting and clapping and leaping like frogs." And bringing up
the end of the procession was a tribe of people like herself, "march-
ing behind the others with great dignity, accountable as they had
always been for good order and . . . respectable behavior. They
alone were on key. Yet she could see by their shocked and altered
faces that even their virtues were being burned away." Mrs. Turpin
knew there was a message in that vision that might somehow
change her whole life and attitude.

By the way, the college girl's name was Mary Grace and
the book she threw at Mrs. Turpin was titled *Human Development.*
Flannery O'Connor had a great sense of humor.

PASSIONTIDE

Matthew 27:45

Tenebrae

It was Holy Week and darkness had fallen upon the monastery
perched atop Graymoor Mountain in the highlands east of
the Hudson River. In the chapel the friars were chanting back
and forth across the aisle the psalms of the ancient rite of
Tenebrae. The Latin word means darkness and the rite, repeated
(at Graymoor) on the three nights prior to Saturday of Holy
Week, laments the death of Christ.

In the chapel sanctuary stood a large triangular candelabrum with seven candles ascending its right and seven its left arm, converging upon a fifteenth candle at its apex. As the friars completed each of the rite's prescribed 14 psalms, an acolyte extinguished one of the candles until only the fifteenth at the top (symbolic of Christ) remained lit. All the chapel electric lights were then also extinguished. A closing prayer was recited and an acolyte lifted the lone candle from its holder and carried it solemnly out of sight behind the high altar. The chamber was now absolutely dark. Silence prevailed. And then (to the surprise of any guests present) all the friars pounded the oaken choir stalls with their heavy hymnals— creating a sound equivalent to thunder itself—to symbolize the cataclysmic nature of what we had done to the Son of God. Only when the echoes had died away was the hidden candle returned from behind the altar and replaced at the top of the candelabrum— to forecast the Good News that the light of life and love can never be fully extinguished, that Christ will rise again and again and again!

As often as I participated in the Tenebrae rite as a young man, I was deeply moved by it. What moved me most was that slow, one by one extinguishing of the 14 candles and the loneliness of that final candle until it too was withdrawn. It seemed to illustrate so poignantly what happens to Jesus in the Passion story: Judas and Peter, Caiaphas and Annas, Pilate and Herod, the mob and soldiers converging on Jesus one by one to quench the radiance of his presence.

And who (I thought) was this cast of characters but you and me! For we play out the Passion story not only during Holy Week but every week of our lives. I mean, the presence of Christ within me struggles with a Judas within me who pretends to love him but really is engaged in arresting his development, handcuffing my Christic potential. The presence of Christ within me looks with sadness upon a Peter within me who's ready to deny him at the drop of a hat if it means sticking my neck out. The presence of Christ within me has to face up to an interminable trial before my Annas and Caiaphas dimensions who insist that he prove beyond a doubt the validity of his Gospel of love before I make any commitment to him. And then there's Pilate, the ambivalent me, who would just as soon wash his hands of the whole affair—and Herod, the voyeur, who likes the promise of miracles but not the hard stuff about turning the other cheek, forgiving one's enemies, caring with all one's heart and mind and strength. And then there's the mob within me, quick to opt for some current fad or TV guru as more compatible to my modern tastes than that depressing figure in crown of thorns and purple displayed on Pilate's balcony.

Yes, for as long as I can remember, Christ's Passion has been billed as "Now Playing" within the theater of my mind, the luminous Christ often reduced to a hardly perceptible taper within the sanctuary of my heart. But thank God for Christ's survival skills! Because the play never quite ends with him simply dead and buried: the acolyte always returns with that solitary candle—this time to start within me (at long last) a conflagration of Pentecostal magnitude?

THE VIGIL IN THE HOLY NIGHT OF EASTER

Genesis 1:1–22, Isaiah 54:5–14, Exodus 14:15—15:1, Herman Melville

The Sign of Jonah

My earliest impressions of Easter include a gigantic rabbit wobbling on a float in an Easter parade, baskets of jellybeans, marshmallow chickens, chocolate eggs, and real ones of blue and pink—all of which had little to do (as I found out later) with Christ's Resurrection and much to do with the pre-Christian cult of *Eastre* (or *Oestre*), the Germanic goddess of spring whose seasonal role was to make the sap rise and flowers bloom and bunnies multiply like crazy. Of course, it has always been Catholic Christianity's genius to "baptize" such pre-Christian cults, to reorient them to celebrate not just a change of seasons but also the rising of Jesus from his tomb.

If I had had a good catechist as I was growing up, she might have offered me an Easter symbol more in line with our biblical heritage—namely, water! Not just the water that comes from the tap. No, she would have led me over to the Mendocino coast of a stormy eventide and pointed to that water—the vast, rolling, pounding sea. And she would have reminded me of the opening lines of our Easter Vigil's first reading from Genesis: "In the beginning . . . darkness covered the abyss while a mighty wind swept over the waters."

The sea: chaotic, bottomless, full of the stuff of nightmares, suffocating! Yet out of this formlessness God in Genesis calls forth sunshine, the stars, the green earth, and all living things, and ultimately you and me, made in God's own image. What a wonderful event, issuing in a Garden of Eden set amid so many galaxies.

But it was a garden that could be swallowed up by the sea again whenever we human beings became nostalgic and ran like lemmings back to the oblivion, the formless "sea" whence we came. The story of Noah, referred to in our Vigil's fourth reading from Isaiah, offers us one instance of such regression. But again, it reveals God's creative intent to resist such recoil, to pluck us out of the waves as he did Noah and set us on dry land, to insist we become God's sacramental presence in this world. Yet no sooner do we emerge from one biblical sea than our third Vigil reading describes us confronted by another, the Red Sea of Exodus, waiting to swallow us anew, until once more we hear, "The Lord swept the sea with a strong east wind throughout the night and so turned it into dry land." Yet again God provided us a highway out of the suffocating waters of regression to stride once more toward a land flowing with milk and honey.

Water, the sea, symbol of death and yet so strangely—under the influence of God's Spirit—the source of life! The same sea into which timid Peter almost sank before Jesus lifted him to safety and a sense of mission. The same sea Jesus could quiet with a word. The same sea out of which he would invite his fishermen friends to draw forth a net full of souls, even as tonight we draw forth new members of the Church out of baptismal waters, out of the mouth of Leviathan, another marine symbol of death.

Speaking of which, the story of Jonah comes to mind. Jesus once said, "Just as Jonah was in the belly of the whale three days and three nights, so will the Son of Man be swallowed up by death, but only to rise again." And who are you and I but Jonah? Jonah was told by God to live bravely, to convert the regressively violent civilization of Nineveh. And what does he do? He behaves regressively himself. He heads out to sea to escape God's summons and ends up in the belly of a whale; he "goes down" (as Herman Melville describes it in *Moby Dick*) "in the whirling heart of such a masterless commotion that he scarce heeds the moment when he drops seething into the yawning jaws awaiting him; and the whale shoots-to all his ivory teeth, like so many white bolts, upon his prison."[15]

Regression! Choosing NOT TO BE! Easter is about the reversal of all that. It's about our choosing TO BE, to emerge from baptismal water, to grasp anew the hand of Jesus, who would restore us to our proud status as sons and daughters of God—this risen Jesus whose own exit from the tomb, whose own escape from the belly of the whale, has had everything to do with our capacity to *breathe* again.

So as you prepare for Easter don't forget to ponder this biblical symbol of water. Remember that Easter fundamentally has to do with our breaching the surface of baptismal water, of overcoming the physical and spiritual power of death to drag us under. It has to do with our experiencing a resurrection akin to that of Christ. It is a resurrection akin to Jonah, so powerfully retold by Melville: "Yet even then beyond the reach of any plummet—'out of the belly of hell'—when the whale grounded upon the ocean's utmost bones, even then, God heard the engulfed, repenting prophet when he cried. Then God spake unto the fish; and from

the shuddering cold and blackness of the sea, the whale came breech-
ing up towards the warm and pleasant sun, and all the delights of
air and earth; and 'vomited out Jonah upon the dry land'; when the
word of the Lord came a second time, and Jonah . . . his ears, like
two sea-shells, still multitudinously murmuring of the ocean—Jonah
did the Almighty's bidding. And what was that, shipmates? To
preach the Truth to the face of Falsehood!" And I might add: to BE
true, to BE real, to BE in the fullest sense of the word. Happy Easter.

SECOND SUNDAY OF EASTER

John 20:19–31

Look before You Leap?

As a member of a research firm many years ago I was part of a team
assigned to produce a consumer guide for homebuyers. The idea
was to get people to look before they leaped, to spend time drawing
up a precise list of their housing needs before making a commitment. The list might include the size of the house, the size of the lot,
the style of house, garage space, ground maintenance, commuter
distances, proximity to schools, quality of schools, proximity to
markets and churches, price, lenders, points, utility costs, crime
rate, future development, and so forth.

In other words, buyers were to spell out every residential
concern they had, even to the point of square footage, mileage distances, and traffic decibels! Of course, once you had people thinking this way it's not inconceivable that they might even want to
inspect the résumés of local elementary school teachers, but we
never encouraged them to go that far. But then again why not?
Because, after all, we were trying to get them to think like researchers,
to go about purchasing things in a scientific way—to diminish
their chances of making a mistake, a bad investment.

Now while the logic behind this approach to home buying was beyond dispute, I don't think our consumer guide had a snowball's chance in hell of being of any ultimate use to most human house hunters. I mean, I could just picture a couple (the wife with a thumb-worn checklist of rational criteria on her lap) turning down a shady lane, coming upon a "For Sale" sign in front of an ivy-covered cottage right out of Peter Rabbit, and exclaiming, "This is it! We love it!" And the basis for their judgment? Not the checklist but the charm of the place, its appeal to a need deep within them that made all their rational requirements irrelevant.

We never produced such a consumer guide for fellows looking for a wife. You know, getting him to develop a similar checklist defining the precise woman he might need to suit his temperament, career ambitions, and so on, like five feet two, eyes of blue, college degree, a touch of Irish, a girl just like the girl that married dear old dad! Again, what would be the use? Love can never be reduced to a science. Into the lobby walks this girl who in no way conforms to the fellow's checklist. She speaks "and the angels sing" and the checklist is last seen bobbing in the wake of a cruise ship en route to paradise.

Thomas the apostle would have loved to be a member of our consumer guide team, because from what we know of him he was the kind who preferred to look before he leaped. He had to see, to touch, to examine those wounds before he would invest in the tale told him by the other starry-eyed disciples. But like all such folk who insist that reality bend to their requirements before they accept it, Thomas felt his checklist slip from his fingers, reduced to a dead letter in the presence of the risen Jesus who confronted him. There's no suggestion that he even thought of inspecting his wounds, for given the depth of his grief over having lost Jesus and his corresponding astonishment at having found him again, Jesus probably looked to him more like the Jesus of the opening chapter of the book of Revelation: "The hair of his head was white as snow-white wool, and his eyes flamed like fire; his feet gleamed like burnished brass; his voice was like the sound of rushing waters; out of his mouth came a two-edged sword and his face shone like the sun."

And what could Thomas say in the face of such a reality, which appealed to a need so deep within him, far deeper than his quibbling mind could fathom? What could he say but "My Lord and my God"?

SECOND SUNDAY OF EASTER
OPTION

John 20:19–31

The Incredulity of Thomas

Way back in the days when all art was sacred art, depicting saints or episodes from the Bible, one of the artists' favorite subjects was the episode described in today's Gospel. Thanks to John Drury's work, *Painting the Word*,[16] I've been recently alerted to a fascinating change in artists' approach to this episode during the sixteenth century. For example, we have in Italy a painting of doubting Thomas's confrontation with Jesus from around the year 1503. At that time all of Western Europe was still united in its faith, loyal to the centuries old Church centered on the Eucharist and the See of Rome. Kings, merchants, and farmers all believed in the great narrative of the Bible, were baptized, confirmed, shriven, married, and laid to rest according to the same rites. True, there had been stirrings of dissent throughout the Middle Ages, but things were still hanging together, sustained by what some today would call a naïve faith.

And so in a 1503 painting (by Cima da Conegliano) the meeting between Christ and Thomas is serenely portrayed. Jesus stands majestically in the center of the painting. His torso is bare, revealing the wound in his side. His color is of an opal whiteness,

his face gently turned toward Thomas on his right. The ten other
apostles (Judas is, of course, missing) are arranged on either side
of him, all their faces relatively in shadow compared to that of the
more mystical Saint John, whose face and bared breast is of the
same opal tone as that of Jesus. But even the rest of the apostles
appear peaceful—even Thomas, who indeed raises his hand
to touch the side of Jesus, but in a posed way as if the artist has
asked him to repeat the gesture well after Thomas has already
said, "My Lord and my God." I mean he looks hardly dubious of
Christ's Resurrection.

But consider another painting of the same episode done
around 1621 by Guercino. Remember that over the intervening
century the faith of Europe had been shaken. The Reformation had
split a once united Europe into two or more camps. The authority
of the popes no longer influenced the minds of kings, merchants,
and farmers. Columbus had discovered new continents. Sailors had
returned from the Far East with news of other ancient religions and
civilizations. Copernicus had suggested that, far from the sun orbiting the earth, it was the earth that orbited the sun. Such revelations
stimulated the curiosity of a once credulous people, giving rise
to a science that would put all old wives' tales out of business forever. Nor was it long before critical minds placed even the Bible
under the microscope to test the validity of its stories. The modern
era was underway.

And so what do we behold when we stand before this 1621
painting of today's Gospel event? Jesus leans backward as if assaulted,
his wound exposed to a darkly bearded and shaggy-haired Thomas
who leans aggressively forward--his face hard, peering at the wound
while his extended fingers probe more like those of a surgeon than
an apostle. Jesus holds in his left hand the white banner of his victory over death, but its folds are blown violently by a wind coming
from the direction of a still unconvinced Thomas. How prophetic
a forecast of our modern era in which even the existence of Jesus
has been called into question!

But may this modern revival of Thomas's incredulity not serve as a blessing? May contemporary incredulity and even ridicule of religious faith on campuses and in the media not compel us to become better informed about what we believe—snap us out of our merely habitual allegiance to our traditions? May it not compel us also to test the depth or shallowness of all those other options sold in the modern market place? May it compel us not simply to possess our faith but to intelligently and behaviorally bear witness to it (as Thomas eventually did), lest generations to come suffer the consequences of a world devoid of any humanly satisfying meaning whatsoever?

THIRD SUNDAY OF EASTER

Luke 24:13–35

Camouflage

My wife and I had just begun to climb the path to the summit of Corona Heights in San Francisco. Corona Heights is a low hill topped by prominent rocks above Market Street that presents the viewer with a grand display of the Mission district, the Bay, and, to the left, the skyline of San Francisco, which on this day in the strange light of a sunless sky looked like a vast Cubist painting, with its rectangular buildings of every size and shade and its Transamerica pyramid. My wife and I go there on every anniversary of our son Philip's death because it overlooks where he lived and died on Duboce Street, and because the last time we saw him we were driving up Market Street and he pointed to the Heights and said that was his favorite place of retreat and if he ever had to live on the streets, that's where he'd stay.

Well, back to our ascent of the Heights last Sunday. To make the climb easier, the park people had cut some steps into the soil at the path's lower reaches and reinforced them with wooden four by fours. We had only climbed a couple of steps when my wife said, "Look, a butterfly." She was pointing directly to the step in front of us. I couldn't see anything, but she insisted there was a stationary butterfly, which had just closed its wings. Of course, that's why I couldn't see it—because with its wings closed the butterfly was so camouflaged we could hardly distinguish it from the soil, pebbles, and sticks at our feet. As she pointed, I looked hard and said, "Where?" And she said, "Wait." And then the butterfly's wings opened and I beheld the sudden splendor of a new monarch butterfly in all its orange, black, red, and white spotted symmetry! It was like an apparition out of nowhere.

It then took flight but only to alight on the next step, where it again folded its wings and became what looked like a sliver of wood. We waited and watched, and again it opened its wings and transfigured the ground and repeated this ritual for several steps upward until I got the message and said, "The butterfly is telling us that Phil is here. We can't see him, but he's here and if he were to open his wings we'd see him in all his splendor." And so we continued our ascent sensing that Phil was with us all the way— camouflaged by death but still present with a transcendent beauty.

Is that not what happened to the apostles after the death of Jesus? I mean, even when Jesus was alive they failed to perceive who he really was. They imposed on him the camouflage of their own presuppositions. Or take the experience of those two disciples on the road to Emmaus after the death of Jesus. Here they were walking beside him, engaging in conversation with him, but did they see him? No, not until he sat with them at table and broke bread and gave it to them. That's when he opened his wings and displayed for a moment the monarch he really was! And so it was with all his apparitions to his disciples. Were they not moments when, by opening to them the deeper meaning of the scriptures, he opened to them the essence of who he really was—the grace of God incarnate? And in opening his own wings throughout all those Resurrection episodes, did he not compel his apostles to lay aside their own camouflage, to open up their own wings, to reveal their own capacity for gracious being? And do not all these Gospel episodes we listen to throughout this Easter season demand that we too lay aside the camouflage by which we conceal (even from ourselves) our own redeemed beauty?

I must say, last Sunday's experience with that monarch butterfly helped me feel (in relation to Philip) something of the joy Mary Magdalene experienced when, assuming the risen Jesus to be only a gardener, she heard him simply say, "Mary"—saw him simply open his wings—and realized he wasn't dead after all.

FOURTH SUNDAY OF EASTER

John 10:1–10, Kenneth Grahame

The Wicket

There are gates and there are gates. Your ordinary gate gives access to your front yard or some fenced-in field. But then there's the gate Kenneth Grahame writes about in his essay "The Fairy Wicket,"[17] which can lead you beyond the ledger books and drudgery of adult survival back to the world you knew so well when you were a child. Wicket is simply a quaint word for gate, and therefore Grahame felt it an appropriate term to apply to that special gate that can conduct us into a world where fantasy reigns supreme.

Of course, in his essay Grahame laments the gradual disappearance of that magic gate as we grow older. It once was everywhere to be found, through which we might behold elfin dances or some prince upon a white charger or meet some chipmunk endowed with speech and wisdom. But then along came schooldays (or "schooldaze") and cheerless classrooms and prolonged hours spent indoors over sums and syntax and the acquisition of skills

geared to make us productive cogs of the business world and—
poof!—the wicket became hardly visible anymore.

Occasionally, Grahame notes, it might seem right around
the bend of some lane on a weekend's excursion in the country or
certainly just the other side of that row of elm trees. You can almost
hear it "swinging to its familiar click." But no, he says, it always fails
to materialize. The landscape remains prosaic. Then again, "a certain bottle of an historic Chateau-Yquem, hued like Venetian glass,
odorous as a garden in June" may conjure up the presence of that
lost gate and beyond it a vision of ancient France and dueling
courtiers and stately ladies. But "Alas! too shallow the bottle, too
brief the brawls: not to be recalled by any quantity of Green
Chartreuse."

But I'll tell you one place you can still find that gateway to a
vision and experience of Paradise! Go visit any ancient cathedral in
Europe that goes back a thousand years and approach its portal.
You'll see no mere door but a work of art that may show, centered
amid sculptures of saints and angels, an image of Mary under the
title *Porta Coeli* (Gate of Heaven). Or you may see a sculptured
Christ up at the top of the portal's arch, swinging wide open the
doorway to his wedding banquet while on his left five foolish
virgins (their eyes heavy with sleep, their lamps extinguished) miss
out on the festival, while on his right five wise virgins stand wide
awake to his invitation and ready to enter his kingdom all aglow.

By such art our ancestors, who built those cathedrals, were
trying to tell us that every cathedral, and therefore the Church itself,
is the magic gateway that can convey us into a more profound experience of life and reality than we might otherwise realize. Their
architecture helps us visualize what Christ in today's Gospel says
of himself: "I am the gate; whoever enters by me will be saved and
will come in an go out and find pasture."

Here ultimately is the magic wicket, the elusive gate
Kenneth Grahame and so many souls seek: Christ and his Christic
way of being. And here's the surprise effect of our passing through

that Christic gate and becoming Christic ourselves: we may now say of ourselves what Christ says of himself: "I am the gate." For whenever we behave in a Christlike way, compassionately and generously, we ourselves become the magic wicket by which others may gain access to God and by which God may gain access to this world to make of it a Garden of Eden once more. You see the gate swings both ways.

FIFTH SUNDAY OF EASTER

John 14:1–12, Francis Thompson

Turn But a Stone

In today's Gospel Jesus says, "In my Father's house there are many dwelling places . . . . And if I go to prepare a place for you, I will come back again and take you to myself, so that where I am you also may be." Where is this "Father's house" of which Jesus speaks? The apostles Thomas and Philip assume it is at some distance from the world in which we live. Thomas says, "Master, we do not know where you are going; how can we know the way?" Philip simply asks for a glimpse of this invisible Father.

Jesus says, in effect, "It's not far away. In fact, you're right on the threshold of it. I myself am the path and, as a matter of fact, whoever has seen me has already seen the Father, for I am in the Father and the Father in me."

Being fragile, feeling unsubstantial and often of little account, we human beings have always assumed that substance, power, and worth lay somewhere else, at some great distance from "poor me." This has led to our literal acceptance of political and religious aristocracies down through the ages. In olden times we assumed kings and nobility were superior; nowadays we look with envy on the rich and famous. And then there were the religious hierarchies, the high

priests of the many temples of the world, superior, "holier," closer
to divinity than we. And of course, ultimately all substance and
worth lay with God, who dwelled at an infinite distance from this
passing world.

Well, the Gospel of John would disabuse us of this nonsense. The heavenly realm, the Father's house to which Jesus is about
to go, is just a step away from Thomas and Philip and us. You can
just reach out and touch it if you want. Our Father's house is simply
the unfolding world that lies just on the other side of our fears
and doubts the moment we let faith and compassion take over
our senses: our eyes and ears and fingertips. The world itself then
becomes a grand temple, a cathedral, and every one of us a priest,
ordained by God to live liturgically within it, to become what an old
hit song called "Poetry in Motion."

Francis Thompson was well aware of this when he wrote his
poem "The Kingdom of God":

> O World invisible, we view thee,
> O World intangible, we touch thee,
> O World unknowable, we know thee,
> Inapprehensible, we clutch thee!
>
> Does the fish soar to find the ocean,
> The eagle plunge to find the air—
> That we ask of the stars in motion
> If they have rumour of thee there?
>
> Not where the wheeling systems darken,
> And our benumbed conceiving soars!—
> The drift of pinions, would we hearken,
> Beats at our own clay—shuttered doors.

The angels keep their ancient places;—
Turn but a stone, and start a wing!
'Tis ye, 'tis your estrangèd faces,
That miss the many-splendoured thing.[18]

SIXTH SUNDAY OF EASTER

John 14:15–21

The Accuser, Who Accuses Us Day and Night, Has Been Deposed (Revelation 12:10)

In the book of Job we are given a clear picture of what makes Satan diabolical. There he sits at God's celestial cabinet meeting. God has just expressed admiration for his earthly servant Job. And Satan sneers, "Sure, Job looks good but how deep does it go? How can you be certain he's not a fraud?" Like Shakespeare's Iago (possibly the most diabolical villain in all literature), Satan stirs the pot. His name means "Adversary" and he exists to accuse us of anything he can ferret out.

And all the while we thought Satan's role in history was to entice us to do wicked things. On the contrary, his role has been to accuse us of evil until we're so browbeaten, we doubt we are of any worth at all, become bilious, desperate and give up—at which point Satan smiles his subtle smile of success.

Of course, you can't see Satan, but he's really present wherever the spirit of accusation dominates our lives. That's just about everywhere, if you read the papers. I mean, before we're five years old, we're being summoned before the tribunal of parents, siblings, teachers, and peers for not measuring up to expectations.

It's not long before the din of such criticism becomes so loud that we internalize it, so that in the absence of anyone else to accuse us, we're quite ready to accuse ourselves: "Why don't you get your life together? When will you ever learn? Where did you get that hat?" Feeling up against the wall under such a barrage of judgment, we lash out, engage in counteraccusations, and pretty soon we're caught up entirely in that battle royal otherwise known as the politics of human experience. And Satan's smile broadens—the spirit of accusation holds us ever more firmly in his closed fist.

The New Testament is about God's decision to break the accuser's enervating grip upon us. Look at the behavior of Jesus in so many Gospel scenes. When questioned as to why he dines with sinners, he says it's because they are ill. You don't drag illness into a courtroom—you treat it with compassion. Again we see him interfering with the execution of a woman caught in adultery. As her advocate he says, "Let him who is without sin cast the first stone."

Again we see him in the house of Simon the Pharisee (who under his breath finds fault with the party crasher at Jesus' feet). "Let me tell you something," says Jesus. "This woman has made mistakes but they carry little weight when balanced against her enormous love. You, Simon, might learn from her by curtailing your criticism just long enough to show minimum courtesy to your guests."

And in the parable about the prodigal son, the forgiving father (embodying the Spirit of Christ) says to his judgmental older son: "Give us a break. He was dead and now he's alive; we lost him and now he's back. Stow the vindictiveness and come, celebrate his existence and your own."

It's because Jesus is aware of the persistent shadow of the prince of darkness, this spirit of accusation that belabors us, that in today's Gospel he promises to send us the Advocate, somebody to stand up for us, to remind us of the grace of God when we feel battered by accusations of failing to measure up. Amid such juridical bedlam we may find consolation in the signals of God's own public defender within us saying, "Don't worry. Your fate will not be determined before the judges of this world, but within the realm of a God of whom Scripture says, 'If God is for us, who can be against us? . . . Who will bring a charge against God's chosen ones? It is God who acquits us. Who will condemn?'" (Romans 8:31–33).

SEVENTH SUNDAY OF EASTER
FEAST OF THE ASCENSION

Ephesians 1:17–23, Jonathan Swift

Seating Him above Every Principality, Authority, Power, and Dominion . . . He Put All Things beneath His Feet

We're all familiar with Gulliver's sojourn among the Lilliputians, a people who stood only six inches tall.[19] We're not so familiar, perhaps, with the reverse experience he had when he found himself among the Brobdingnagians, who averaged 70 feet tall! There he stood in a field of wheat 40 feet high, while a line of Brobdingnagian reapers approached wielding seven-foot sickles. Realizing he could be squashed under foot or cut in two, Gulliver screamed as loud as he could, whereupon one of the reapers stopped short. He looked at Gulliver as we might view a mouse and then bent over, picked him up, and held him within three yards of his eyes.

The Brobdingnagians treated Gulliver gently as a curiosity. Eventually he was able to converse with their king and boast about England's empire and political institutions. He failed, however, to realize that this gigantic king could evaluate all Gulliver said from a much higher vantage point. And so, far from being impressed by Gulliver's account of English history, the king was appalled. To him it appeared to be nothing but a petty "heap of conspiracies, rebellions, murders, massacres, revolutions, banishments, the very worst effects that avarice, faction, hypocrisy, perfidiousness, cruelty, rage, madness, hatred, envy, lust, malice and ambition could produce." He could only conclude Gulliver's countrymen "to be the most pernicious race of little odious vermin that nature ever suffered to crawl upon the surface of the earth."

Embarrassed by this assessment, Gulliver tried to impress him with the achievements of European science and technology, inventions such as gunpowder and cannonballs (and we might add hydrogen bombs). This too left the king amazed at "how so impotent and groveling an insect . . . could entertain such inhuman ideas." He then ordered Gulliver, if he valued his life, never to mention these things again while in his kingdom. Gulliver privately ridiculed the king's reactions as shortsighted, forgetting that it was he who was short and therefore shortsighted in this land of benign giants.

This brings us to this matter of Christ's ascension. In our creed we say of Jesus: "For us and our salvation he came down from heaven." We believe that Jesus came into our world possessing a much higher vantage point from which he could well perceive how small we are and how small we often behave—our human pettiness and its often vicious consequences. He came to unmask these limitations, to lift us up out of all this lethal pettiness and myopia, to share with us his higher and therefore more profound vision of reality, his bigness of mind and heart.

"And when I am lifted up from the earth, I will draw everyone to myself," he says in John's Gospel (12:32). And Saint Paul plays upon this same theme in his letter to the Ephesians, where he prays that we may all "comprehend what is the breadth and length and height and depth" (3:18) of Christ's way of loving, where he speaks of our attaining a maturity measured by nothing less than "the full stature of Christ" (4:13).

And have you ever noticed how often Jesus takes his disciples up to a mountain top—to pray, to deliver his Sermon on the Mount, to be transfigured before them, to be elevated on his cross (which becomes for us our ladder to heaven), and finally to carry our gaze even higher as he ascends into the heavens themselves? He does this all in an effort to entice us toward a taller, wider, all encompassing, compassionate view of things—to make of us a race of spiritual giants similar to those Gulliver met in Brobdingnag.

PENTECOST SUNDAY

Acts 2:1–11, John 20:19–23, Eudora Welty

On Our Dryness Pour Thy Dew (Pentecost Sequence)

The Holy Spirit or creative breath of God arrives among us in a variety of ways. For starters, its presence is described in Genesis 1:1 as a mighty wind sweeping across a formless abyss, summoning light, sky, land, and life into being. Or again, in the book of Exodus it issues from the bosom of God as a strong east wind, piling up the waters of the Red Sea to allow the Israelites to emerge from Egypt and begin their journey toward a land flowing with milk and honey. And then there's today's description of the Spirit's descent on the apostles, sounding like a strong driving wind and manifest in tongues of fire, symbolic the Spirit's intent to set the whole world on fire with love.

On the other hand, the Spirit may come in gentler ways as in today's Gospel in which the risen Jesus simply breathes upon his anxious disciples and says, "Peace be with you." And then there's that touching account of the same Spirit's descent upon Mrs. Larkin as narrated by Eudora Welty in her brief story "A Curtain of Green."[20]

Every day one summer (Eudora writes) it rained a little. But on this particular day the daily ration of rain had not come. As late as five o'clock the sun was still ablaze; everything seemed metallically hot. Women of this small Mississippi town sat by their windows fanning themselves. Only Mrs. Larkin remained active, spending all her time working her garden despite the warmth.

Ever since her husband accidentally died the year before, she would enter her garden every morning and work away aimlessly at the soil, planting "every kind of flower she could find or order from a catalogue." She would plant quickly, carelessly, without regard to arrangement or even harmony of color. "And if she thought of beauty at all . . . she certainly did not strive for it. . . . It was impossible to enjoy looking at such a place. To the neighbors gazing down from their upstairs windows it had the appearance of a jungle."

Mrs. Larkin didn't care. Neither gardening nor life really had any meaning for her now. True, at times she did feel something flutter within her breast like some bird struggling to fly free, but she always lapsed into a deep depression. Then under the sun, her hair uncombed, all she could do was keep "chopping in blunt, rapid, tireless strokes. Her eyes were dull as if from long impatience or bewilderment. Her mouth was a sharp line. People said she never spoke."

How well that describes so many us in our modern world who, bewildered by disappointment or death, become skeptical of any deeper meaning to things. And what is there left for us to do but keep busy: hoe that garden, punch that clock, turn that channel, develop that property, widen that existing highway to take us nowhere new. It's enough to drive anyone mad!

And angry is what Mrs. Larkin became on that arid afternoon. It was the whistling and faraway smile of her helper Jamey, "the colored boy who worked in the neighborhood," that got to her. What right had he to smile? What right had he to dream, to contemplate some "flickering and beautiful vision" when she beheld only emptiness? She took tight hold of her hoe and approached Jamey as he bent over his work. She raised the hoe slowly in silent anger to strike out at this dark angel and his music, his ridiculous dream, and this ridiculous universe. But then Eudora writes:

> In that moment, the rain came. The first drop touched her upraised arm. Small, close sounds and coolness touched her.
>
> Sighing, Mrs. Larkin lowered the hoe. . . . She stood still where she was, close to Jamey, and listened to

the rain falling. It was so gentle. It was so full—the sound of the end of waiting.

In the light from the rain, different from sunlight, everything appeared to gleam unreflecting from within itself. . . . The green of the small zinnia shoots was very pure, almost burning. One by one, as the rain reached them, all the individual little plants shone out, and then the branching vines. The pear tree gave a soft rushing noise, like the wings of a bird alighting. . . . A wind of deep wet fragrance beat against her.

Then as if it had swelled and broken over a levee, tenderness tore and spun through her sagging body.

It has come, she thought senselessly . . . against that which was inexhaustible, there was no defense.

Mrs. Larkin fainted. Jamey ran and crouched beside her. In a beseeching voice he called her name, "Miss Lark'! Miss Lark'!" until she stirred. And so the story ends. But who can doubt that beneath that gentle rain—symbolic, too, of how God's Spirit works within our lives—whatever it was she had felt flutter within her breast was finally set free?

PENTECOST SUNDAY
TOPICAL: VENI, SANCTE SPIRITUS

Sequence

I have what must now be a collector's item. It's the 1954 English translation of Pius Parsch's five-volume commentary on the Liturgical Year.[21] When published it sold in paperback for $2.75. It may read a bit archaic today because the liturgy has changed a lot since then, but his quarto-sized work remains loaded with good information about the history of the Mass as well as edifying commentary. And what I want to share with you are his reflections on the hymn called the sequence in the Mass for Pentecost.

This hymn (which in Latin began *Veni, Sancte Spiritus*) is very ancient. Indeed there used to be many such sequences woven into liturgies in the Middle Ages. People loved to compose and sing them. But after the 1570 revision of the Roman Missal, only a handful were retained. Now Parsch informs us that the sequence for Pentecost is no loosely contrived composition. It's a five-stanza piece tightly built on the short phrase "Come, Holy Spirit, fill the hearts of your faithful," which you will find located between the alleluias sung prior to the Gospel.

And how does this Sequence relate to that alleluia phrase? Well, each of its stanzas expands on one of the words in the phrase: Come—Holy Spirit—Fill—The Hearts—Of Your Faithful. Thus:

Come:

> Come, Holy Spirit, come!
> And from your celestial home
> Shed a ray of light divine.
>
> Come, Father of the poor!
> Come, source of all our store!
> Come, within our bosoms shine.

Holy Spirit:

> You, of comforters the best;
> You, the soul's most welcome guest;
> Sweet refreshment here below;
>
> In our labor, rest most sweet;
> Grateful coolness in the heat;
> Solace in the midst of woe.

Fill:

>O most blessed Light divine,
>Shine within these hearts of yours,
>And our inmost being fill!
>
>Where you are not, we have naught,
>Nothing good in deed or thought,
>Nothing free from taint of ill.

The Hearts:

>Heal our wounds, our strength renew;
>On our dryness pour your dew;
>Wash the stains of guilt away:
>
>Bend the stubborn heart and will;
>Melt the frozen, warm the chill;
>Guide the steps that go astray.

Of Your Faithful:

>On the faithful, who adore
>And confess you, evermore
>In your sevenfold gift descend;
>
>Give them virtue's sure reward;
>Give them your salvation, Lord;
>Give them joys that never end.
>Amen. Alleluia.

How's that for taking five words and—as Jesus did with a few loaves and fishes—multiplying them to produce a wonderfully nourishing prayer? Perhaps meditating on this sequence can be your way of experiencing the presence of the Holy Spirit today, as did the disciples of long ago—as a breeze sweeping through your soul, as a tongue of fire bright within your heart.

THE MOST HOLY TRINITY

Exodus 34:4–9

Good Things Come in Threes

In our first reading for today from Exodus, the Church seems to find a hint of God's being a Trinity, for God, having come down from a cloud, repeats his name three times: Lord, Lord, Lord. Now a modern biblical scholar may suggest we're stretching things a bit to find the Father, Son, and Holy Spirit of subsequent Christian tradition in so thoroughly Hebrew a book as Exodus. And I'm willing to concede the point. But the threefold repetition of God's name in today's passage does set me off on another inquiry. Why does the number three pop up so often in the Bible?

For example, Noah, after sailing around in his ark, sends out a bird three times to see if the waters have subsided—and on the third try the bird brings back evidence of land. Again, three is the number of Noah's sons from whom the three branches of the human race known to the Hebrew author descended. Three is also the number of the great patriarchs, Abraham, Isaac, and Jacob. And three is the number of the angels who come to inform Abraham that his aged wife will have a son called "Laughter."

Moving further into biblical history, we meet the hero Gideon who is told to reduce his huge army to a mere three hundred men (a multiple of three) before he can put the invading Midianites to flight. Then there's the story of the boy Samuel, whom God calls in the night three times before he recognizes the voice and is anointed God's prophet. Elijah's history is not without some threes as well, as when he throws water three times upon the altar of sacrifice before calling down fire from heaven to impress the prophets of Baal. And as when he stretched himself three times on the body of a widow's dead son and on the third try brought him back to life.

And there's more! How many days was Jonah in the belly of the whale? Three! And how many were the children thrown into the fiery furnace by wicked King Nebuchadnezzar? Three—who remained unharmed while they sang away in the company of a celestial companion.

Carrying over into the New Testament we meet the Magi, whom the medieval Church assumed to be three in number and viewed them as representing the three phases of life: youth, middle age, and old age. And do you recall how it was "on the third day" that Jesus performed his first miracle at Cana and how, after hanging three hours on the cross, it was "on the third day" that he rose from the dead? And do you remember how, when he ascended Mount Tabor, he took with him three disciples (the same three he took with him into the Garden of Gethsemane) and how Peter, seeing Jesus flanked by Elijah and Moses, wanted to put up three tabernacles there?

It was this same Peter who denied Jesus three times and was then put to the test after the Resurrection when Jesus asked him three times: "Do you love me?" Nor is Saint Paul without a tendency to arrange things in threes, as when, at the end of his wonderful poem on love, he says, "And so there remain these three: faith, hope and love." This finally brings me back to that other threesome whose festival we celebrate today—of whom Jesus says at the end of Matthew's Gospel: "Go therefore and make disciples of all nations, baptizing them in the name of the Father and of the Son and of the Holy Spirit."

What can we make of all these biblical threes? One could speculate for hours and still be unsure. But one thing does stand out. In practically all the biblical episodes in which the number three occurs, something wonderful happens. Noah finds land. Abraham and Sarah have a son. A widow's child is restored to life. A transfiguration takes place. Water is changed into wine. Jonah is regurgitated by a whale. Jesus rises from his tomb. Three children survive a fiery furnace. And Peter learns how to say, "I love you."

So whatever meaning scholars may allow regarding the three-fold utterance of God's name in our first reading, I'm impressed enough by the frequency of the number three in the Bible to revive my old Christian custom of saying the Angelus three times a day (at dawn, noon, and eventide)—just to be in tune with the apparently triplicate nature of our spiritual universe!

THE MOST HOLY BODY AND BLOOD OF CHRIST

Deuteronomy 8:2–3, 14–16, Isak Dinesen

Do Not Forget the Lord Who Fed You Manna in the Desert

There's nothing like a dinner party to draw people together. After a glass of wine and a bit of mingling, the laughter begins amid intense conversation at this or that end of the table. People begin to tell stories out of their past or reveal silly things they've done that they're no longer shy about. Table, food, and drink create a magic that makes of once isolated individuals a community of something close to brothers and sisters. People become frankly affectionate. They let down their guard.

I remember the effect of such dinners upon the members of a religious community I knew. Most of them had known each other for years. They had shared dormitories, refectory, chapel, and class rooms for so long that they knew each other's qualities and faults. There were the jolly types, the brooders, the intellectuals, the con-servatives and liberals, the pinochle players, and the ultra-pious—a mixed bag that over time harbored resentments, formed cliques, gossiped about each other. There were Thomists who were wary of biblical scholars and vice versa and papalists who suspected ecumenists and vice versa.

But along came May and their annual formation gathering in New York, and a miracle took place. After a few days of formal

talks and heated debate (often fueled by the personal dislike of
Father X for Father Y or the way Father Z snidely responded to
what he thought was a stupid question), they would all assemble in
the upper banquet room of an Italian restaurant near Washington
Square. After only one round of manhattans and a taste of antipasto,
they suddenly became a band of brothers, candidly amused by their
collective faults! Overly serious intellectual adversaries now lam-
basted each other playfully with humor and tears in their eyes.
Cliques got reshuffled. The pious few began to smile with pleasant
guilt at the scandalous remarks of their more irreverent confreres.
What I'm trying to say is that conviviality—love—had taken over
as dinner, in some sacramental way, revived their deeper feelings of
solidarity and kinship.

Isak Dinesen's story "Babette's Feast" reveals the same
phenomenon. Perhaps you've seen the film version. Babette is a
French refugee who comes to this cold Norwegian town to work as
cook for two aging sisters who belong to an austere religious sect.
Whenever its members get together, they resemble the Israelites of
today's first reading, a collection of folk who have somehow become
lost in a "vast and terrible" spiritual desert. They all dress in gray
and black, they speak little, and they've renounced all the pleasures
of this world. Behind their facade of piety they engage in petty
quarrels and backbiting; they perpetuate resentments. And they are
desperately in need of manna from heaven, which begins to descend
on them when Babette, having won a lottery, offers to make them
a French dinner.

They accept her offer reluctantly, vowing among themselves
to discipline their sense of taste. But to no avail! After a bit of
Amontillado and pleasant portions of turtle soup, Blinis Demidoff,
Cailles en Sarcophage, and other items washed down by Veuve
Cliquot 1860, two women who held a grudge begin to recall how
as children they used to fill their village roads with song. Two men,
one of whom had long ago cheated the other, began to laugh over
the incident as if it had been a practical joke. Another old couple,

burdened with guilt over an affair of their youth, gave each other a long overdue kiss of reconciliation.

> Of what happened that evening nothing definitely can be stated. None of the guests later on had any clear remembrance of it. They only knew that the rooms had been filled with a heavenly light, as if a number of small halos had blended into one glorious radiance. Taciturn old people received the gift of tongues; ears that for years had been almost deaf were opened to it. Time itself had merged into eternity. Long after midnight the windows of the house shone like gold, and golden song flowed out into the winter air.[22]

No wonder Jesus chose a supper as his sacramental way of passing on his legacy to the world—a supper we perpetuate at every Eucharist. What better ambiance within which to promulgate his only commandment: "Love one another. Nurture one another. By this will all know you are my disciples, by your constantly candid and convivial love."

THE MOST HOLY BODY AND BLOOD OF CHRIST
TOPICAL: EUCHARIST

Marcel Proust

They Knew Him in the Breaking of the Bread

Toward the end of Marcel Proust's masterpiece *In Search of Lost Time* the main character, Marcel, is depressed. He had hoped to be a writer, but the more immersed he became in the decadence of early twentieth-century Paris, the less inspired he felt. Then came the Great War and the loss of friends.

Saddened and recovering from a long illness, he received an invitation to a concert at the home of the Prince de Guermantes.

He arrived late and was ushered into the library to await the end of the performance. The butler brought him some orangeade. After a sip he wiped his mouth with the napkin and instantly a vision of lavender blue passed before his eyes. He sensed the fragrance of salt air. For a moment he thought someone had opened a window on a beach (although he knew he was in Paris). And then it struck him. It was the starchy texture of the napkin! It reminded him of the texture of the towel he had used when as a boy he looked out of the hotel window at Balbec and saw the ocean for the first time. Out of the folds of that napkin he had re-experienced sacramentally "the plumage of an ocean green and blue like the tail of a peacock." The vision lifted him out of his despair. It revived his conviction that there was so much more to life and reality than the social and political rut of Paris.

Things like that had happened at other times to Marcel, as when one day the taste of a madeleine dipped in tea reminded him not only of the tea-soaked madeleines his aunt used to give him as a boy in Combray but of every delightful nook and cranny of the village in which she lived. No doubt you have had similar experiences.

In my case it's the smell of boiling pitch. No matter where I may be, its aroma recalls my boyhood neighborhood of Brewery-town, where roofers frequently mended the row houses on our block. And thereupon follow remembrances of playing marbles for keeps and hopscotch on the sidewalks and collecting wads of matchbook covers (which was all the rage among boys back then) and the thunderstorms in summer when we all donned bathing suits and ran splashing up and down the gutters like Gene Kelly in *Singing in the Rain*. And our neighborhood sandlot team with "Brewerytown" woven in blue across the chests of those older boys—who would one day go to war.

And the coal chutes rattling Koppers Koke into our cellars where you might also find a Victrola with records of Sousa from 1915—and old nasal comedy routines like "McGinty Takes the Census." And the two by fours that became skate boards once you tacked roller skates to the bottom and an orange crate on top. And then it was up to the top of Thirtieth Street hill to descend at terrific speed and brace yourself for a teeth shattering experience at the bottom where the smooth asphalt gave way to the cobblestones of Jefferson street!

And the ghostly breweries (empty since Prohibition) that we used to explore at night! And my grandmother's tea sets, one English and one Japanese. And the Sunday drives along the Schuykill River with my father crooning Hawaiian melodies. And then there was Peggy Dean! And notice how it's always the beautiful, exciting, playful impressions that remain—not the poverty of the times or the schoolyard bullies or the shadow of death.

Many centuries ago Jesus broke bread and gave his disciples wine to sip and said, "Do this in remembrance of me." He knew that down through the ages our struggle to survive might so preoccupy us that we might begin to doubt life's ever being meaningful. And so he gave us this sacramental opportunity—called the Eucharist— to recall how once upon a time an invincible beauty and grace did walk this earth and remains with us still—just beyond the veil of our forgetfulness and despair.

SECOND SUNDAY IN ORDINARY TIME

1 Corinthians: 1:1–3, A. N. Wilson

A Word in Defense of a Very Dear Friend

I often think that Saint Paul must wince every time the Church decides to snip out a verse or two from his letters for our Sunday edification—isolated quotations that hardly do justice to the full scope of his teaching. And he must especially wince when they're taken from his letters to the Corinthians—because the Corinthians were a very special case, like the denizens of the detention room at any local high school. I mean the Christians of Corinth were Paul's worst headache.

Corinth was a Greek seaport and commercial town similar (on a smaller scale) to modern Manhattan. In his 1997 book *Paul, the Mind of the Apostle*, A. N. Wilson describes it as "a place of proverbial wickedness, energy, riches, noise."[23] As the worship center of Aphrodite, the goddess of love, the very word Corinth became synonymous with sexual license, much the way Las Vegas has become synonymous with gambling.

There were cosmopolitan merchants reluctantly subordinated to Roman bureaucrats, both of which rested on a foundation of slaves. Out of all these ranks the Corinthian Church attracted converts, though they did not leave their class prejudices behind. In addition, there was this sectarian spirit among them. Several early Christian preachers came through Corinth besides Paul, such as Apollos and Peter. And no sooner did they pass through than fan clubs began to bicker over who was more orthodox or liberal, dull or fantastic. One could go on about their often trivial disputes over celibacy versus marriage, straight talk versus tongues, and whether it was more appropriate to serve kosher meat than the juicier stuff sold at pagan markets. And, of course, there was all that high dudgeon about somebody having an affair with his stepmother!

Paul preferred to write about higher things—to broadcast Christ's revelation that God is not a sour, litigious God but a God of absolute grace who would have us transcend our differences and experience the joy of mutual graciousness, who would have us experience the relief and energy that comes of knowing that God is the most affectionate parent we shall ever know, whose only concern is that we each become ever more beautiful and productive of beauty down through all eternity.

But when it came to the Corinthians, we find Paul (in effect) saying, "I want to speak to you of the Spirit but how can I when you behave like infants unready for solid food?" And so, descending to their level, he has to fall back upon a long series of elementary or traditional do's and don'ts. The result? People tend to remember Paul only "as a puritanical presence in the Christian tradition. They blame him for taking the simple religion of Jesus and institutionalizing it, or theologizing it, or somehow making it more restrictive."

But Wilson (who is not a Church theologian but a secular British writer) says, "A reading of the . . . authentic writings of Paul . . . absolutely contradicts such a view. Paul is the greatest libertarian of religious history." And to underscore Paul's true genius, Wilson then cites a passage from Corinthians itself which soars so far above and beyond the petty preoccupations of the Corinthian church—words that (if he had written nothing else) would have guaranteed Paul's reputation "as one of the most stupendous religious poets and visionaries the world has ever known." I refer to that passage that begins: "If I speak in human and angelic tongues . . . . And if I have the gift of prophecy and comprehend all mysteries and all knowledge; if I have all faith so as to move mountains, but do not have love, I am nothing."

THIRD SUNDAY IN ORDINARY TIME

Matthew 4:12–23, A. E. Housman

Loveliest of Trees, The Cherry Now . . .

Ours is a questing civilization. Unable to sit still, mariners sailed out of European ports 500 years ago to seek a route to the Indies only to discover America instead, which attracted further endless exploration over the subsequent four centuries. Then they went probing around the tip of South America, ventured into the vast Pacific, and circumnavigated the globe. Having then arrived at every destination on the face of the earth and dispelled the mysteries thereof, their descendants have aimed their ships skyward to probe new frontiers in space.

From where do we derive this need to keep mobile, to cross horizons? Well, scholars will say it's a result of the Bible's influence on the psyche of Western civilization. For what is the Bible but one story after another about people called to pull up stakes and travel to some distant promised land? There's old Noah whose ark was the forerunner of the Santa Maria. There are Abraham and Sarah, who were told to "go to a land I will show you." There's Moses, who led the Israelites across a sea and desert toward a land flowing with milk and honey. Then came Joshua and visionaries like Elijah, Isaiah, and Joel, whose very names were appropriated by the pioneers who forged the Oregon Trail. And there is Jesus who opens these Gospels of Ordinary Time with an invitation to "come after me; join my procession!" With such a heritage, no wonder our civilization has been a mobile, questing one.

But, you know, when you get to be 60 or 70 or so, having passed so many milestones of one kind or another—romance, career, habitat, crises—it's hard to keep up that questing spirit. You run out of gas or curiosity. It seems like there's nothing really new in the news, politics, or vacation options. Lots of new gadgets, yes, but the sales pitch is still the same. Even the spirited hymns and motivational homilies at church fail to accelerate one's pace toward the promised land, given the heaviness of our feet, the weariness of our hearts.

But, hey, what are we complaining about? If we're slower than we used to be, maybe it's a sign that for us the quest is over, a sign we've begun to arrive where God has always wanted us to be, namely in the here and now! Maybe arriving has never been a matter of locomotion but of vision, of simply opening our eyes to the kingdom of grace and beauty all around us, which until now has been nothing but a blur because of our compulsion to be always on the go to somewhere else, some other time.

I mean, when Jesus said, "Come, follow me," was he inviting us to join him in some physical trek from here to there, or was he inviting us to adopt his way of seeing and experiencing things? Was he inviting us to see the world and everyone around us not hastily, on the run, but with a reverence that can slow us down enough to see what Christ and Saint Francis and Renoir and Shakespeare saw— and Mother Theresa, who saw in the outcasts of Calcutta a worth equivalent to that of any Brahmin, Boston, or otherwise? If this be what Christ meant when he said, "Come, follow me," then why rent deckchairs on the Santa Maria when all we have to do is open our hearts to experience the "America" or whatever other "Promised Land" we seek?

A. E. Housman suggests that even those still in the spring-time of life should beware of bypassing God's already present kingdom. Aware the cherry trees were blossoming, he wrote:

> Now of my threescore years and ten,
> Twenty will not come again,
> And take from seventy springs a score,
> It only leaves me fifty more.
>
> And since to look at things in bloom
> Fifty springs are little room,
> About the woodlands I will go
> To see the cherry hung with snow.[24]

FOURTH SUNDAY IN ORDINARY TIME

Matthew 5:1–12

Beatitude

Some people were no doubt offended when the Monty Python film *Life of Brian* made light of the Sermon on the Mount by having hard of hearing persons walk away wondering what Jesus meant by "Blessed are the Greeks" and "Blessed are the Cheesemakers." But even a correct hearing of what Jesus said would suffer ridicule nowadays, given the kind of environment we live in. Liberals might find issue with any suggestion that poverty and persecution can be a blessing, while tough-minded conservatives might be appalled at statements like "Blessed are the meek" and "Blessed are the merciful." And, of course, the "fun" crowd would find "Blessed are they who mourn" absurd.

In an age when athletes and other celebrities and their agents are praised for demanding multimillion dollar salaries, when the media display the rich and famous for our emulation, when corporate "downsizing" is promoted as the profitable and therefore logical thing to do (despite its actually meaning tragic layoffs), who wants to hear anyone advocating poverty of spirit? In an age when pundits shout at each other on TV shows, when the airwaves are loud with boasting, ridicule, and even hatred—when the dominant dogma of society seems to be "Look out for #1, don't take anything from anybody, push your way to the top and nice guys always lose," who wants to listen to talk about meekness, simplicity, kindness, and compassion? Such values would be laughed off the stage.

No, Christ's beatitudes seem really out of date, naive in this sophisticated age of materialist individualism. The beatitudes of this age seem to be:

> Blessed are the avaricious
> Blessed are those whose life is one big party
> Blessed are the arrogant, who take no guff from anybody
> Blessed are those who are fed up with talk about justice
> Blessed are the tough (and cursed be all "bleeding hearts")
> Blessed are the devious
> Blessed are the contentious
> Blessed are they who know precisely who the "bad guys" are
> and are not hesitant to blow them away verbally if not literally

How much more gutsy are those beatitudes compared to Christ's:

Blessed are the poor in spirit (whose happiness depends on something more profound than dividends and limousines)

Blessed are they who know grief and are the wiser for it

Blessed are gentle and considerate folk

Blessed are they who will never be satisfied until they are truly just and decent people

Blessed are the merciful, people who know how to forgive

Blessed are the simple folk, who look you in the eye and speak from the heart

Blessed are the peacemakers

Blessed are they who quietly put up with ridicule for adhering to these beatitudes

But wait a minute! Christ's beatitudes—now that I compare them—seem more like a ticket to a saner world and future than those pugnacious ones. The latter set seem to be merely an echo of "values" that have devastated landscapes and lives since Cain killed Abel and Lamech took pride in avenging himself 70 times seven times. That's old stuff! Christ's beatitudes out of date? On the contrary, they're the only ones that offer us a future worth living for.

FIFTH SUNDAY IN ORDINARY TIME

Matthew 5:13–16, Thomas Mann

Mountain Climbing

As long as I've lived in the Sonoma Valley, I have yet to climb to the top of Hood Mountain overlooking Kenwood. I have approached it several times but have never come close to the summit. The reason?

I've never made the commitment. I've looked wistfully at its rocky pinnacles; I've ascended some of its lower trails, only to rationalize myself downhill with "Well, that's enough exercise for today." But I've never jumped out of bed of a sunny day and said, "This is it! My number one priority today is Hood Mountain. I'm determined to reach the top and take in the view!"

The same may be said of my commitment to climb Saint Matthew's Mount of the Beatitudes. Now there's a summit of far more astounding vistas than one will ever see from Hood Mountain. And it's been standing there above the valley of my soul throughout my life. Indeed, it stands there once again, confronting you and me in the Gospel selections over these few Sundays. But I've yet to defy gravity to that degree, to expand my heart, to breathe in and out that summit's atmosphere of heroic largesse, to participate in Jesus' larger vision of life, people, and human destiny that climactically.

All of this reminds me Thomas Mann's novel, *The Magic Mountain*, which tells of a lad named Hans Castorp, a engineering school graduate employed in his family's steamship business. He was urbane, self-indulgent, and as shallow in his interests as the landscape around the wealthy port of Hamburg. Upon receiving news that his cousin Joachim had been admitted to a tuberculosis sanatorium in the Alps, he set aside two weeks to pay him a visit. He took a train up from the flat seacoast of Germany and over gentle hills and dales until he reached Switzerland. Here he had to change to a narrow gauge track—and now began "the thrilling part of the journey, a steep and steady climb that seems never to come to an end. . . . [as] the wild and rocky route pushes grimly onward into the Alps themselves."

Here he found the air thinner and himself underdressed for the chill of the afternoon.

> This being carried upward into regions where he had never
> before drawn breath . . . began to work upon him, to fill
> him with a certain concern . . . . Perhaps it had been ill advised

of him, born as he was a few feet above sea-level, to come immediately to these great heights, without stopping at least a day or so at some point in between . . . . The train wound in curves along the narrow pass . . . . Water roared in the abysses on the right; on the left, among rocks, dark fir-trees aspired toward a stone grey sky. . . . A magnificent succession of vistas opened before the awed eye, of the solemn, even phanatas-magorical world of towering peaks . . . vistas that appeared and disappeared with each new winding of the path.[25]

This whole novel, of course, is more than a travelogue of Hans Castorp's physical journey into the Alps. It is rather a metaphor of a spiritual ascent that, upon his arrival at his cousin's sanatorium, will last not two weeks but seven years! During that time he will discover he has a soul, transcend his bourgeois complacency, and share the life of the residents of the sanatorium. And ultimately, while lost as a solitary skier in a snowstorm, he will experience a vision of the very kind of world Jesus presents to us from Matthew's mountain—a world in which love prevails even over reason and people never allow the thought or fear of death to bridle their capacity for goodness and love.

Now that's an encouraging story, isn't it? Enough to make me think maybe it's about time I stopped procrastinating. Maybe it's about time I snapped out of it and dared probe the upper reaches, explore the vast vistas of that mountain whose ascent I have put off for far too long. Hood Mountain? No, I'll get around to that sooner or later. I'm referring to Christ's mountain from which he invites you and me to stand and shine beside him, a light to all the world.

SIXTH SUNDAY IN ORDINARY TIME

Matthew 5: 17–37, Mark Twain

You Have Heard It Said: Thou Shalt Not . . . but I Say . . .

While Huckleberry Finn and his runaway companion, Jim, drifted down the Mississippi River, Jim had been able to avoid capture by roaming bounty hunters. Then one day, after Huck had left Jim alone on the raft by the riverbank, Jim was caught and held for possible transfer to the Deep South! When Huck found out, he was not only desolate but also filled with remorse. He began to regret that he had helped Jim escape from Miss Watson up in Missouri in the first place, because she certainly would have treated Jim better than whoever else might get hold of him.

It just went to show (he thought): it doesn't pay to break the law. Missouri law said Jim was Miss Watson's property, and helping Jim escape to the free states was simply stealing somebody's property—and stealing was an offense against God. "The more I studied about this," he mused, "the more my conscience went to grinding me, and the more wicked and low-down and ornery I got to feeling. And at last . . . it hit me . . . here was the plain hand of Providence slapping me in the face and letting me know my wicked-ness was being watched all the time from up there in heaven. . . . Well, I tried the best I could to kinder soften it up somehow for myself . . . but something inside of me kept saying, 'There was the Sunday school, you could a gone to it.'" Finally he tried to relieve his guilt by writing a note to Miss Watson telling her exactly where she could retrieve Jim. This made him feel a lot better. It's never too late to obey the law and avoid hell while you've still got breath![26]

But then Huck got to thinking about Jim and their trip down the Mississippi. He thought fondly of their conversation, their singing, and their laughing. He thought of how "I'd see him stand-ing my watch . . . 'stead of calling me, so I could go on sleeping;

and see him how glad he was when I came back out of the fog . . . and would always call me honey . . . and do everything he could think of for me, and how good he always was." And Huck then looked at that note and wondered if should he send it, if should he do the right thing or the wrong thing by Missouri law. He held his breath and then said, "All right, then, I'll go to hell"—and he tore up the note. He figured that if caring about Jim's freedom was wicked by Missouri standards, then "I would take up wickedness again . . . . And for a starter, I would go to work and steal Jim out of slavery again; and if I could think up anything worse, I would do that, too; because as long as I was in, and in for good, I might as well go the whole hog."

What Huck didn't realize at that moment is that Jesus would have admired his decision immensely, because Huck was beginning to realize that some of society's laws can actually get in the way of true love. He might have even been on the verge of realizing that even good laws—even the law of Moses—establish only a minimal standard of decency. And as such they can be spiritually dangerous, because people may settle for that minimal standard as the maximum required of them! That's precisely the point Jesus tries to make in his Sermon on the Mount. "I tell you, unless your righteousness surpasses that of the scribes and Pharisees you will not enter into the kingdom of heaven"—you shall never know how profoundly delightful a heroically generous life can be.

The Church, under the pressure of history, sometimes lowers its expectations to the minimal; it promulgates all sorts of do's and don'ts to accommodate people's need for a recipe of behavior. But, insofar as the Church still teaches the Sermon on the Mount, deep in her heart she would rather we be so much more imaginative, spontaneous, ultra-compassionate, as gracious as God himself when it comes to morality. The Church would have us go maximal rather than minimal—or, if she were to adopt the jargon of that barefoot saint, Huck Finn, she might say, "If you're going to be good, you might as well go the whole hog!"

SEVENTH SUNDAY IN ORDINARY TIME

1 Corinthians 3:16–23, Anne Porter

Do You Not Know that You Are the Temple of God?

The Old Testament can't seem to make up its mind about temples. One moment God seems opposed to them. When David wants to build one in Jerusalem, God gets angry and effectively says, "Who do you think you are? Do you think you can confine God to some holy of holies, some sacred box within real estate boundaries set by you? I am the Creator of the universe. The whole universe is my shrine; I am present in every part of it. And you want to box me in like some pet parakeet so you can control me? I won't stand for it." So David backed off.

But along came his son Solomon, who revived the idea and apparently this time God said all right and took up his abode within the tight quarters reserved for him—I guess as a concession to Israel's need to house its God as ornately as other nations housed theirs. Still, you get the impression God was a reluctant guest, annoyed by the smoke of animal sacrifices behind which the Israel's aristocracy might conceal its lack of ethics. God's annoyance gets expressed in the oracles of his prophets in terms like "I've had enough of burnt offerings; I don't delight in the blood of bulls; I'd rather have you seek justice, correct oppression, defend the fatherless." When the situation failed to improve, God finally said, "I'm leaving!" and allowed the prophet Ezekiel to witness his departure as a radiant cloud drifting off through the east gate of the city into the wide open spaces of the Arabian desert—after which invading Babylonians leveled both Jerusalem and its temple.

Still, up went another in which Israel assumed God would concede to dwell again. And then one day along came Jesus, who within the Temple courtyard itself dared to refer to his own body as God's temple, thereby triggering the idea that every individual is

God's temple, that the sacred is present everywhere—in each and everyone of us—so that Saint Paul can say of us in today's second reading, "You are God's temple; the Spirit of God dwells in you." And Saint Peter can say elsewhere that the true temple of God is our community of faith, whose members are its living stones.

And yet we Christians still like to build sanctuaries. But we do it in a different spirit. For us a cathedral like Chartres is not to be seen as an exclusively holy place within an otherwise profane world. On the contrary, it's meant to exhibit by way of its sculptured saints, columns, vaults, and stained glass windows what God's whole universe must look like to one who has faith. Chartres does not contradict the holiness of the sky, stars, forests, mountains, and manifold creatures of the world; rather, it displays them artistically within its own precincts so that when we exit we may better comprehend the whole universe to be God's grand cathedral within which we must walk and behave reverently.

That's how Anne Porter felt after visiting the place with its forest of praise and constellations and lancet windows and the great North Rose, "whose blue is blue as blood is red whose red is radiant." Her reaction before this gem of the thirteenth century?

> Father you have allowed us
> For once you have permitted us
> To make a thing so beautiful
> As to be no less beautiful
> Than your own Creation.[27]

EIGHTH SUNDAY IN ORDINARY TIME

Isaiah 49:14–15, Kenneth Grahame

The Secret Drawer

In one of Kenneth Grahame's episodes in *The Golden Age*, the boy-narrator tells of his being introduced by his uncle to a remote room—a kind of attic—in his aunt's house. Among the things stored there was an old writing desk. "H'm! Sheraton!" remarked his uncle, referring to the desk's eighteenth-century make. He then let down the flap to reveal the desk's many pigeonholes and drawers. "Fine bit of inlay," he said, "good work, all of it. I know the sort. There's a secret drawer in there somewhere."[28] The uncle then left the room, but the boy's whole being was set to "vibrating to those magic syllables—a secret drawer." They conjured up images of a sliding panel, bullion, ingots, Spanish dollars, and hidden treasure. The boy thought of all the things he might do with such treasure: buy a pipe for the local shepherd, pay back Edward the four pence he owed him, buy young Harold a toy battleship (the HMS Majesty, now lying in dry-dock in the toy shop window, just when her country had some need of her). And then there was that boy in the village who had a young squirrel he was willing to sell for one shilling. The boy had "wants enough to exhaust any possible find of bullion, even if it amounted to half a sovereign."

In quest of this treasure the boy later returned to the room alone and approached the desk. He let down the flap and with expectant fingers "explored the empty pigeon-holes and sounded the depths of the softly-sliding drawers." He let his fingers probe every smooth surface in search of some knob or spring that might release the secret drawer—but all in vain. Unyielding, the old desk stood stoutly guarding its secret. He grew discouraged and paused to lament his bad luck. This wasn't the first time Uncle Thomas had proved shallow, uninformed, a guide into blind alleys. But try again he must, and hardly had he put his hand "once more to the obdurate wood, when with a sort of small sigh, almost a sob of relief, the secret drawer sprang open."

Excited, he carried the drawer to the light by the window. But his excitement gave way to disappointment, for the drawer contained no ingots or silver but only two tarnished gilt buttons, a crayoned picture, some foreign copper coins, a list of birds' eggs and where they had been found, and one ferret's muzzle. Nothing of any worth at all! And yet, as the boy viewed the drawer's contents, a warmth crept back into his heart, for he knew them to be the hoard of some long forgotten boy like himself—treasures "he had stowed away . . . one by one, and . . . had cherished . . . secretly awhile: and then—what? Well, [thought the boy,] one would never know why these priceless possessions still lay unreclaimed; but across the void stretch of years I seemed to touch hands a moment with my little comrade of seasons—how many seasons?—long since dead."

Don't we all have a secret drawer somewhere that contains things, worthless to everyone but ourselves? In my own house we have a secret closet full of toys, bedtime storybooks, a silent guitar, and even a guitar pick of my lost son that are worth more to me than all the tea in China. And if we no longer have some literal secret drawer somewhere, don't we all have one deep within our psyches, filled with personally joyful and tragic memories, hurts and hopes, a cherished anxiety or two, and perhaps no little remorse? Don't we all have an inner sanctum that no one else knows or even cares about?

Except that God does. Isn't that what our first reading for today tells us: that no more than a mother can forget her child, neither can God forget you. For God knows all about that inner sanctum within each of us that somehow makes each of us a "person" and not a statistic. And, of course, the sooner we ourselves, like the boy in our story, become as sensitive as God to that inner sanctum in others, the sooner we will begin to see each other as kindred souls and treat each other with reverence and concern:

I restored the drawer, with its contents, to the trusty
bureau, and heard the spring click with a certain satisfaction.
Some other boy, perhaps, would some day release that
spring again. I trusted he would be equally appreciative.

NINTH SUNDAY IN ORDINARY TIME

Romans 3:21–25, 28

Manifesto

Saint Paul wrote his letter to the Romans in 58 AD while passing
through the Greek city of Corinth. He had not yet been to Rome
to visit the Christians living there. His work until then had been
limited to the eastern side of the Mediterranean. Now he was eager
to preach in its western region, even as far as Spain, and hoped to
make Rome his base of operations. But he sensed a problem. The
Roman Christians might be wary of him because of rumors they
had heard.

You see, there were certain Christians back then, possibly
former Pharisees like Paul, who followed him from town to town
badmouthing him. "Watch out!" they might say. "This Paul fellow
has gone off the deep end! His take on Christianity is too radical,
irresponsible! He speaks of God as a God of absolute grace, mercy,
and compassion, and no longer as that fulminous Judge we've
known so well, with his rules and regulations, which are the only
recipe we have to avert his wrath and win his favor."

These Christians were reluctant to give up their former
pharisaical principles. They wanted to keep the New Testament
"Old." They found a certain security in those kosher food laws and
other practices whereby they could distinguish themselves from the
profane world around them. What would become of society if all
these props, along with the concept of God as overseer and judge,

were to give way to a God of absolute mercy! The classroom would go wild; people would simply sin with abandon, if only to allow God ample opportunity to be even more merciful.

Well, if that's what the Romans had been hearing, Paul had better write to clear the air—in a letter outlining his faith and its logic. "Look around you," he writes. "The pagan world is sinning without let up: greed, envy, murder, meanness, arrogance, selfishness everywhere. And now look at the so-called pious, who think that because they live under a judgmental God and possess his laws they have some guarantee that they can live proper lives and merit God's reward and avoid his wrath. What do you see? Be honest. You see the same greed, arrogance, selfishness, and treachery. So! If God is to remain the strict Judge you cherish, who's to escape his wrath. Nobody! By the logic of this juridical notion of God we are all doomed.

"Unless there is an alternative vision of God! And that's precisely what Jesus came to reveal—his Parent and ours, a God of mercy, compassion, gracious intervention, who simply wants intimacy with each of us that we might inhale his expansive Spirit, transcend fear and dare to behave divinely. And do you fret that belief in a God of absolute grace will undermine morality? Do you hesitate to trust, to believe? Do you hesitate to step from your traditional life raft onto the waters where Jesus walks?

"Well, I guarantee you this. Once you experience God as a God of grace, who cares intimately and absolutely about you, who's not out to frighten you the way human patriarchs do, who sees compassionately through your errors to the fear that produces them and longs to relieve your fear, supplant it with a new sense of worth— once you experience this, you may not go hog-wild at all like some kid when school lets out! Experiencing grace and compassion, you may in fact enjoy it so much, find it so contagious you will yourself become gracious and compassionate and thereby arrive at a level of morality far beyond what any scribe or legal system expects of you. By that I mean a spontaneous, authentic, imaginative morality that's more like art than labor. Now that's my Good News and Christ's Good News! And as far as I'm concerned, nothing short of it will ever make any sense to me."

~~~~~~~~~~~~~~~~~~~~~~~~~~~

TENTH SUNDAY IN ORDINARY TIME

Hosea 6:3–6, John Steinbeck

It Is Love that I Desire, Not Victims

So now that Christ has been born (way back at Christmastime) and grown up and made his way up to Jerusalem (all through Lent) and died and gone to heaven on Ascension Day, where does that leave us? Well, if you consult your Missal, it leaves us in what the Church calls "Ordinary Time," which seems to say: right back where we started from, trekking our way through the long hot summer of history, un-dramatically laying one foot down in front of the other as we advance toward the autumn of our lives, toward uncertainties looming like a dark horizon ahead.

I've been noting a lot of similarity lately between the lives we live and that famous trek of the Okies from the dustbowl of the 1930s toward what seemed like the Promised Land of California— as told by John Steinbeck in *The Grapes of Wrath*. Talk about uncertainties! Like the Hebrews of the biblical Exodus, these down-to-earth Americans were buffeted by hope one minute and confusion the next as they ran into people coming the other way saying they'd rather starve in Oklahoma among friends than starve in a hostile California. Their used cars break down and highway merchants behave like highway bandits! Why carry on?

Of course, "why" can be the worst question to ask in a crisis. That's how Tom Joad felt at times. When Casey, the defrocked preacher, says, "Well—s'pose all these here folks . . . can't get no jobs out there," Tom replies, "I'm jus' puttin' one foot in front a the other . . . . This here bearing went out . . . . Now she's out an' we'll fix her. . . . This here little piece of iron and babbit. See it? Ya see it? Well, that's the only goddamn thing in this world I got on my mind."[29] Nor does Uncle John care much for speculation: "I don't think nothin' about it. We're agoin' there, ain't we? None of this here talk gonna keep us from goin' there. When we get there, we'll get there. When we get a job we'll work, an' when we don't get a job we'll set on our tail. This here talk ain't gonna do no good no way." Hooray for Uncle John. Sometimes speculation about the whys and wherefores of life becomes a good excuse for ignoring immediate obligations—like living.

But Casey represents another dimension of ourselves that needs to see the big picture, to figure out where we've been, to get a sense of direction about where we're headed—in other words, what's the meaning of all those journeys of peoples past and present and of you and me down through the seemingly ordinary times of our lives. Casey thinks they add up: "They's stuff goin' on and they's folks doin' things. Them people layin' one foot down in front of the other, they ain't thinkin' where they're goin' . . . but they're all layin' 'em down in the same direction . . . . An' if ya listen, you'll hear a movin', an' a sneakin', an a rustlin', an'—an' a res'lessness. They's stuff goin' on that the folks doin' it don't know nothin' about—yet. They's gonna come somepin outa all these folks goin' wes'—outa all their farms lef' lonely. They's gonna come a thing that's gonna change the whole country."

As an ex-preacher, Casey shares something of the hope expressed in today's reading from Hosea, a sense of the Holy Spirit working in history as quietly as the dawn or a spring rainfall, fashioning a world in which mutual victimization has finally given way to a divine ethic of mutual mercy and love.

In the absence of an ascended Jesus, there are moments when no such vision seems likely. But Steinbeck has this way of signaling the presence of a divine undercurrent shaping our destiny, as when Mae, the waitress at a road stop, looks wistfully after a poor family that's just left and asks the short order cook Al: "I wonder what they'll do in California?" "Who?" says Al. "Them folks that was just in," says Mae. And when Al replies, "Christ knows," we know he's not just uttering a profanity. Because we know that Christ does indeed know and, thanks be to God, he's let us know—in a profound way—what life is all about.

<hr />

TENTH SUNDAY IN ORDINARY TIME
TOPICAL: SACRAMENTS AND SACRAMENTALS

Sublime Opportunities to Decelerate

In Italy it seems customary to sing the *Salve Regina* in Latin at the end of Mass. It's a plaintive piece of ancient chant that my generation learned to recite at school in English, ending with the words: "O clement, O loving, O sweet Virgin Mary." Hearing it also brought back memories of monastery evenings when we friars sang the anthem in a darkened chapel before going to bed. And so it remained familiar enough for me to join in with congregations in Ravello and Perugia and savor its phrases like *Ad te suspiramus gementes et flentes in hac lacrimarum valle* (To thee do we send up our sighs, mourning and weeping in this valley of tears).

And there were indeed times on our recent trip to Italy when I did feel like sending up sighs, mourning and weeping in this valley of tears, as when occasionally the ATM machine would spit back my card, saying "Illegible" or "Call your bank." Or when a hotel clerk would run my Visa card through his machine and hand me a slip of paper that said, "Authorization denied." Apparently somebody at my bank was dismayed by evidence of my cards' being used in Italy instead of Sonoma and started pushing buttons to save my account from some thief. But the thief was me—and I needed cash! Without cash hotel clerks can quickly change from friendly to chillingly formal—and an intended vacation can become an ordeal.

But my uneasiness throughout our trip was not simply fiscal. It was also metaphysical. Thanks to last year's experience, I was better able to maneuver through Italy by car—not only over its highways but also through the narrow, winding streets of mountainside towns a thousand years old. But what this meant was that we were bound to experience more things than we could possibly absorb in three weeks. One day we walked amid the ruins of Ostia Antica, the next day we stood before the Coliseum and surveyed the Forum of Rome itself, and the next day we walked through the ruins of Pompeii.

At another moment we were immersed in the atmosphere of Ravello, with its eleventh-century cathedral and fifteenth-century villas and its boast of having been the temporary residence of Richard Wagner and D. H. Lawrence. At another we were eating beneath the arched brick ceiling of a cistern from the time of Augustus Caesar or exploring the interior of a Romanesque church that dated from the year 1200 or a baroque church from 1600 or a palazzo that housed Joseph Bonaparte. We stood in squares dedicated to the nineteenth-century hero Garibaldi, looked with wonder at the frescoes of Giotto in Assisi, and then passed through Etruscan gates over 2,000 years old to merge on freeways with trucks from every corner of modern Europe.

In other words, the tour became a barrage of sensations so that at times I felt as though I were cascading down a vast river of time not knowing "where" or "when" I had been yesterday and anxious about my whereabouts tomorrow, given the fickleness of those sphinx-like ATMs.

It's at such moments that you find yourself reaching out for something solid to hold on to—as in Perugia when I said to Jane one day: "I've got to see those paintings of the Annunciation and Nativity and the Adoration of the Magi at the museum. I've got to see those thirteenth-century faces of Mary and the angels and shepherds and kings, to live for a moment within their golden frames and know what it's like to feel eternal."

And then, of course, there was the Eucharist at which I experienced Jesus reaching down to me as to a sinking Peter and chiding, "O you of little faith, why do you doubt? You're in Italy. Enjoy it!" But especially there was that *Salve Regina*, which is a plea to Mary for help whose very melody becomes evidence of her presence, delivering a peace no piece of plastic ever will—whether it works or not.

ELEVENTH SUNDAY IN ORDINARY TIME

Exodus 19:2–6, James Joyce

You Shall Be for Me a Kingdom of Priests

> —To receive that call, Stephen, said the priest, is the greatest honor that the Almighty God can bestow upon a man. No king or emperor on this earth has the power of the priest of God. No angel or archangel in heaven . . . has . . . the power of the keys . . . the power of exorcism, the power to cast out from the creatures of God the evil spirits that have power over them, the power, the authority, to make the great God of Heaven come down upon the altar and take the form of bread and wine. What an awful power, Stephen![30]

These words of the spiritual director of Belvedere College in Dublin were not without effect on Stephen Dedalus in James Joyce's autobiographical story *A Portrait of the Artist as a Young Man.* "A flame began to flutter on Stephen's cheek as he heard in this proud address an echo of his own proud musings." But Stephen eventually resisted the director's invitation. Fundamentally, he wanted to be a poet and had come to believe that poetry and priesthood were incompatible callings.

How sad, because priests are supposed to be gatekeepers to realms holy and sublime—to a vision of the world so much more real and profound than our everyday world of compulsive, terror-driven reflexes and moods. Their role is to reveal that sacred panorama we all long for as an alternative to a fallen world of lone-liness and continual parrying with others. Their function is to reveal that panorama by word and gesture, by creating sacramental happenings that actually evoke experiences we might call celestial. But unfortunately Stephen ran into a few priests in his early years who seemed to have had no inkling of what their calling was about. For instance, there was that retreat master whose sermon on hell covers 27 pages and is well worth reading before a mirror if you want to watch your hair stand on end.

No, for Stephen priesthood seemed to have more to do with rules, rubrics, warnings, the repression of vitality and vision—and so he sought an alternative route to a sublime, creative engagement with life and its mysteries. He left the Church to become an artist. He left the Church, whose heritage from the imagery of the Old and New Testaments down through the chants of Citeaux, the master-pieces of Giotto and Dante, and the splendor of its cathedrals is so laden with poetic expression and visions sublime.

Of course, had their lives overlapped, chance might have brought Stephen into contact with another late nineteenth-century priest in Dublin named Gerard Manley Hopkins, who had an eye for beauty that might have convinced Stephen that priest and poet were not incompatible callings. A priest who could write such things as

> Glory be to God for dappled things; . . .
> Fresh-firecoal chestnut-falls; finches' wings.[31]

Let's face it. Everything Stephen's spiritual director said about the priesthood is descriptive of a poetic vocation as well. Both may claim the "power of the keys" to open our eyes to dimensions we so often miss; to drive the evil spirits of greed and pettiness from our hearts; to reveal the presence of God in bread and wine, in dappled things, in finches' wings, in Leopold Bloom, and "the sea crimson sometimes like fire."

Aren't we as a Church meant to be a kingdom of priests according to today's first reading? And, as such, aren't we also then expected to become poets, artists—makers of songs and things delightful, doers of deeds divine?

TWELFTH SUNDAY IN ORDINARY TIME

Matthew 10:26–33, Seamus Heaney, Denise Levertov

Digging

The first poem in the Irish Nobel Prize winning poet Seamus Heaney's most recent edition of poems is titled "Digging." Why? Because that's what modern poets do. They dig for meaning. Like the scientist or philosopher who strains to resolve the mystery of life and nature, the poet, too, in this modern era of confusion, tries in his or her imaginative way to uncover the hidden origin and direction of human experience.

In this particular poem, Heaney recalls how so much of his father's time was spent literally digging into the bogs of Ireland. What an art it was!

> The coarse boot nestled on the lug, the shaft
> Against the inside knee was levered firmly . . .
>
> By God, the old man could handle a spade.

And so could his grandfather:

> My grandfather cut more turf in a day
> Than any other man on Toner's bog. . . .

Nicking and slicing neatly, heaving sods
Over his shoulder, going down and down
For the good turf. Digging.

The cold smell of potato mould, the squelch and slap
Of soggy peat, the curt cuts of an edge
Through living roots awaken in my head.

Heaney, as a poet, then goes on to say:

But I have no spade to follow men like them.
Between my finger and my thumb
The squat pen rests.
I'll dig with that.[32]

Jesus would have been very sympathetic to Seamus Heaney's use of digging as a way of describing humanity's quest for the fundamental truth of things, because here and there throughout chapters 10 to 13 of Matthew's Gospel Jesus often refers to the truth he preaches as something hidden. He compares the kingdom of God to a mustard seed or to a bit of yeast hidden within three measures of flour, or to a priceless pearl hardly visible upon a counter of junk jewelry, or to a treasure buried in a field. And it's that same mysterious treasure that all poets, scientists and philosophers dig for—whether they're aware of it or not—by way of their often shortsighted investigations and imaginations. Indeed, today many, ignorant of the clues offered by our Gospel tradition, despair of ever discovering why there is a world or why we exist except eventually to die.

But the elusiveness of God's cosmos of grace has nothing to do with God's cosmos of grace. That reality is quite apparent to those who have become gracious enough to believe in it. It's the overlay of our misconceptions, preconceptions, biases, and paranoia that bury the cosmos alive! But alive it remains, waiting for Jesus

to resurrect it day after day, waiting for those who share his vision
to proclaim it from the housetops. This is what saints and good
preachers and sound social activists—and, yes, children and good
poets—do, like Denise Levertov, who in her poem "Primary
Wonder" confesses:

> Days pass when I forget the mystery.
> Problems insoluble and problems offering
> their own ignored solutions
> jostle for my attention, they crowd its antechamber
> along with a host of diversions, my courtiers, wearing
> their colored clothes; cap and bells.
>
>   And then
> once more the quiet mystery
> is present to me, the throng's clamor
> recedes: the mystery
> that there is anything, anything at all,
> let alone cosmos, joy, memory, everything,
> rather than void: and that, O Lord,
> Creator, Hallowed One, You still,
> hour by hour sustain it.[33]

With such poetic testimony, plus the dependable testimony
of the faithful who show up in our pews every Sunday, may we not
hope that the truth about our world (which has remained concealed
from so many since the gates of paradise closed upon an obstinate
Adam and Eve) may one day be universally revealed?

TWELFTH SUNDAY IN ORDINARY TIME
TOPICAL: BELONGING

A Picture's Worth a Thousand Words

Some time ago, a classmate of my sister in Philadelphia called to tell me she had a photo I might like to have. It was of a group of 31 Resurrection parish altar boys (ranging from the sixth to the eighth grade) taken on a picnic in the summer of 1939. Well, I remembered that picnic—a day of games, swimming, and barbecue hosted by Father Monville on the rural campus of a local seminary. I remembered especially the eats and almost drowning Father Monville. But I couldn't remember any picture being taken. So I said, "Yes, send me a copy."

Now you have to know that I attended Resurrection parochial school for only three semesters. Actually, my elementary school experience reads like a litany: St. Cyril's, St. Ludwig's, King of Peace, then back to St. Ludwig's, then Resurrection, and finally St. Matthew's. Six schools in eight years. The reason? Mainly economic. Upon my registering (usually in the middle of a semester), I was led into my appropriate grade's classroom, subjected to the skeptical gaze of about 40 other children, and introduced as "so and so, who will be joining us . . . and I want you all to make him feel at home." At that remark the skeptical look on the boys' faces changed to one of latent sadism, a transformation that escaped the nun but was very evident to me, because I had been through this ritual several times before.

It usually took about a week before the schoolyard "initiation ceremonies" were exhausted. Then followed the cultivation of a few pals, significant eye contact with a redhead named Rosemary, enrollment in the altar boys—and so on, until my parents decided to move to another neighborhood before I could ever really say, "Gee, at last I belong!" The result? In my later years I could never quite get over a sense of unresolved distance between myself and whatever group I might associate with. I retained this feeling of always being on the outside looking in.

Within a week, a manila envelope arrived addressed in Mary Jane's still-liquid Palmer script. I opened it and there we all were, laughing, arranged in three rows, standing, sitting, or squatting in the trampled grass—the Nolans, Kelley, Murphy, Corkery, Turco, the Vearling brothers, Tomlinson, Callahan. Some had tattered baseball mits; some were in undershirts, or no shirts at all, hair mussed. And there I was in the front row, second from the right, smiling too, flanked by my friends, Bill Miller and Joe Whylie (now dead these many years).

And as I looked at my 11-year-old face, it seemed to be saying to me, the viewer, "What are you doing out there all by yourself? Why do you continue to suffer the illusion you didn't belong? Can't you see you were very much in the picture? Don't you remember how, amid all the moves your parents made, it was you who insisted on going to a school named St. Somebody? Why? Because in some unconscious way you found there in that atmosphere of the Church, among the sisters and classmates and the saints that bedecked the walls, a circle of cultural solidarity that made you feel at home in ways this world will never quite understand. It doesn't matter how many schools you went to or how briefly you stayed—because I, your 11-year-old self, can testify: you did find family—as in these everlasting faces of your fellow acolytes with whom you shared that rare capacity to say in Latin: *Introibo ad altare Dei: ad Deum qui laetificat juventutem meam* (I shall go up to the altar of God . . .)— the God who gladdened your childhood days."

THIRTEENTH SUNDAY IN ORDINARY TIME

Matthew 10:37–42, Charles Dickens

Whoever Loses His Life for My Sake Will Find It

> "Now Joseph Gargery, I am the bearer of an offer to relieve you of this young fellow your apprentice . . . ."

> "I am instructed to communicate to him . . . that he will come into a handsome property. Further, that it is the desire of the present possessor of that property, that he be immediately removed from his present sphere of life and from this place, and be brought up as a gentleman— in a word, as a young fellow of great expectations."[34]

The young man in question was Philip "Pip" Pirrip, the main character in Charles Dickens' novel *Great Expectations.* No sooner were these words of Mr. Jaggers spoken, than Pip's heart began to beat wildly. For he had been aspiring to become a gentleman ever since he had been sent as a boy to perform odd services at the local mansion of the elderly Miss Havisham.

Pip lived with his sister and her physically strong but spiritually gentle husband Joe Gargery, the village blacksmith. As a child of limited means he was content enough. He was in fact your typical wide-eyed boy, having no particular demands on life. And he loved Joe very much, admiring his nonjudgmental, openhearted approach to life in general. But then came this opportunity to experience the environment of the upper class, to walk within the grounds and corridors of a great estate, to meet Estella, the lovely but condescending niece of Miss Havisham.

Suddenly everything about his home and environment seemed coarse. He began to make distinctions. Joe now became an embarrassment to him. Upward mobility became his aspiration. Like the builders of the Tower of Babel, Pip assumed that to be truly

secure one must somehow transcend lower class anonymity. He
believed this despite the fact that the people he met at the top were
hardly happy. Despite their wealth and polished language, they were
a vindictive lot, cold-hearted, competitive, hardly comparable to the
only true "aristocrats" in the novel, our gracious blacksmith Joe and
Biddy (Joe's wife after Pip's sister died). So Pip, upon hearing that
some unknown benefactor wanted to support his ascent, was
overjoyed to leave the forge behind and go up to London.

Well, Humpty Dumpty had a great fall. Pip's fortunes eventually collapsed. He came to discover that his benefactor was not
Miss Havisham (as he had supposed) but an escaped convict to
whom he had once given food as a child. Torn now between his initial
disgust at the thought of such a patron and compassion for his
patron's plight (he was not supposed to be in England and could be
hanged if caught), Pip chose compassion, left his perch willingly,
and recovered all those virtues that make us truly rich.

One could say he underwent a kind of rebirth, became
again, but in a more conscious way, the simple, refreshing child
he had once been before ambition and self-interest polarized his
life. Dickens suggests this in a highly symbolic scene at the close
of the novel. There, Pip, chastened and possessed of a more tender
heart, returns to visit Joe and Biddy on an evening in December
(always a time of rebirth).

> . . . I laid my hand softly upon the latch of the old kitchen
> door. I touched it so softly that I was not heard, and looked
> in unseen. There . . . as hale and as strong as ever though
> a little grey, sat Joe; and there, fenced into the corner with
> Joe's leg, and sitting on my own little stool looking at the fire,
> was—I again!
>
> "We giv' him the name Pip for your sake, dear old
> chap," said Joe, delighted when I took another stool by the
> child's side . . . "and we hoped he might grow a little bit like
> you, and we think he do."

FOURTEENTH SUNDAY IN ORDINARY TIME

Romans 8:9, 11–13, Isak Dinesen

If You Live according to the Flesh, You Will Die . . .

I'm not sure about you, but growing up in some way spoiled things
for me. I can still remember as a child seeing my first iris, hearing
the ice cream truck come down the street, tasting vanilla, smelling
my grandfather's aftershave—and just enjoying the experience.
I asked no questions; I needed no explanations. Every scene, sound,
taste, and scent was fascinating.

The same was true about stories I heard, tales of talking
geese and mice, of giants and buried treasure, or episodes from
the Bible like Noah and the ark, Moses and the Red Sea, Jonah and
the whale, Jesus walking on the water. They all captivated my
imagination and introduced me to a world even wider and more
wonderful than the actual dandelions at my feet—a world
transparent with Spirit.

But then I grew up and was taught to disengage from my
environment and ask questions. For instance, what's the aerody-
namics of a butterfly? How many light years away are the stars of
the Big Dipper? Why did God make me? What makes a ball bounce
up and down? Who really wrote Hamlet? All legitimate interests,
but as a consequence I found myself living more in a world of
explanations, not immediately savoring an iris but classifying it.
I was living in a world that Saint Paul would call a world of mere
flesh. I mean, whereas once I loved to hold a clammy, pulsating frog
in my palm, now I was given a dead one to trace the why and how
of its guts amid the reek of formaldehyde.

I think one unconscious reason I went off to the seminary
in the middle of my high school career (not long after the frog
experience) was to find my way back beyond the useful whys and
wherefores of modern life to the more immediate, personal, spiritual

experience of creation I had as a child. But even there in the seminary I found myself spending most of my time in a classroom. For, you see, even though our tradition derives from the poetry of the Bible, from the Holy Spirit's lively accounts of people for whom the experience of God and creation was immediate and intimate, it wasn't long before we began to probe the why and how of all that too. A perfectly legitimate enterprise, but there I was once again caught up in a world of heavy abstractions.

We spent more time analyzing the nature of Christ in Platonic or Aristotelian terms than experiencing him, more time naming and ranking the angelic choirs than being angelic. Even in that more sacramental environment, while my head became fully stocked with doctrinal slogans about God and salvation, my heart kept wondering, "Why do I feel so alien and empty, so uninspired?"

Then came the break! I was sent on to major in biblical studies. Suddenly I found myself passing beyond the abstract tomes of my seminary days to immerse myself critically and aesthetically in all the Holy Spirit's profound accounts of creation, the flood, Abraham's wonderful trek to fullness of life, Joseph's coat of many colors, the miracles of Jesus. I let myself be carried away by Job's whirlwind to experience the universe as God sees it—as a poet. I savored the parables of Jesus. Gradually I found myself recovering something of that intimacy I had as a child with the unfathomable yet so familiar mystery of life. I even began to appreciate all that dry theology I had been taught because now I was in touch with the fundamental drama it was trying to explain, the Spirit who could bring it all back to life.

Cardinal Salviati, that great character in Isak Dinesen's *Last Tales,* tells a penitent, "Madame . . . . Stories have been told as long as speech has existed, and *sans* stories the human race would have perished, as it would have perished *sans* water."[35] This is simply a way of repeating the basic message of the Bible itself: "In the beginning was the Spirit and without God's Spirit, God's breath, all flesh must perish."

FIFTEENTH SUNDAY IN ORDINARY TIME

Matthew 13:1–23, Evelyn Waugh

Sightings

"Oh dear, it's very difficult being a Catholic," complained Sebastian Flyte, the son of an old aristocratic English family that had remained Catholic since the days before Henry VIII.[36] Sebastian was addressing Charles Ryder, a fellow Oxford student and friend, whom he had invited to vacation at his family's estate called Brideshead.

Ryder was a polite agnostic who looked upon religion as pious nonsense—a hobby which immature people professed but enlightened people did not. And he wasn't really surprised by Sebastian's remark over the difficulty of being Catholic, because Sebastian was hardly a practicing Catholic. For one thing, he drank too much. So Charles replied, "I suppose they try and make you believe an awful lot of nonsense?"

"Is it nonsense?" mused Sebastian. "I wish it were. It sometimes sounds terribly sensible to me."

"But my dear Sebastian," pressed Charles, "you can't really *believe* it all. I mean about . . . the star and three kings. And in prayers? You think you can kneel down in front of a statue . . . and change the weather?"

"Oh yes," said Sebastian. "Don't you remember last term when I took Aloysius [his Teddy Bear!] and left him behind I didn't know where? I prayed like mad to Saint Anthony . . . and immediately after lunch there was Mr. Nichols at Canterbury gate with Aloysius in his arms, saying I'd left him in his cab."

I think what Eveyln Waugh is trying to show in his novel *Brideshead Revisited* is how odd or schizoid we Catholics may appear in this day and age to people of more recent vintage. We are as modern as the next person. We accept the findings of science as far as they go. We are in fact physicists, doctors, astronauts, engineers.

We admit that comets have tails millions of miles long. And yet we persist in believing that a personal Creator (someone not unlike us) explains this great universe and not just a Big Bang. We believe this Creator remains in touch with us and is behind every human Exodus from bondage to real freedom, and that this Creator became present among us in Jesus whom we ineffectually killed because he would have us love rather than despise one another.

And so we can understand why Sebastian says he finds it difficult to be Catholic—to be caught up in two different worlds: one that prefers a skeptical approach to life and one inclined to give things seemingly fabulous the benefit of the doubt. At one point Ryder admits that Catholics at times do seem the same as other modern folk. But Sebastian plaintively protests, "My dear Charles, that's exactly what they're not . . . they've got an entirely different outlook on life; everything they think important is different from other people. They try and hide it as much as they can, but it comes out all the time."

The Charles Ryders of this world will continue to say, "How can you believe all that; there's no scientific evidence of God; no one has ever seen God." But since when has the human eyeball become the final arbiter of what exists or doesn't exist? And insofar as the God of our Gospels has been ultimately identified with Love, doesn't God become sublimely visible every time a human being behaves with compassion? Such sightings of God have been happening since the dawn of history and will continue to occur whenever love compels a human ego to explode with beneficence.

SIXTEENTH SUNDAY IN ORDINARY TIME

Matthew 13:24–43, William Shakespeare

"So Fair and Foul a Day I Have Not Seen"

The play *Macbeth* begins with three witches chanting the words: "Fair is foul, and foul is fair. Hover through the fog and filthy air." What could they possibly mean? I think they're trying to impart a bit of wisdom. They're simply saying: "What may appear or sound fair today may turn out to be foul; and what may appear and sound foul today may turn out to be quite fair after all."

Now that's very confusing. Most people like fair to remain fair and foul to remain foul, right to be right and wrong to be wrong, good to be good and bad to be bad. We prefer a world of clear-cut distinctions so that we may make our way through life safely amid polarizations that have become familiar, permanent. In other words, we don't like ambiguity, we don't like living in a world of "fog and filthy air." We want reality to adapt itself to the "equations" we set up, so that true stays true and false will never surprise us by someday becoming true. How else can we control our destiny, maintain our sanity?

But the three sisters warn us to be ready to find in what we think "fairness" something possibly foul and in what we're convinced is "foulness" something probably fair! For instance, in the play Macbeth and Banquo win a battle on behalf of King Duncan who is delighted with that fair outcome. Fair outcome? Duncan will be dead within 24 hours, foully slain by the hand of Macbeth! Macbeth himself is earlier promised a fair future: he's told he will first become a baron and then King, bright prospects that turn out to be fraught with dark consequences.

So I think Shakespeare, by way of his three witches, is trying to wean us from hard and fast "absolutes" and "opinions" by which we would arrange the world—for example, that my interpretation of history must be the standard by which all other interpretations should be judged right or wrong.

"Judge not," says Jesus, "that ye be not judged," which is a way of saying, "Suspend judgment. Wait. Let the truth emerge out of the fog that envelops us. Let's not drag it out into the open in some partisan way only to find out we've strangled somebody in the process." Think of the parable of the tares whereby Jesus tells those who would rip out the weeds from the wheat: "Suspend judgment. Let the weeds and the wheat grow together. Leave all judgment to God." And I think Jesus was wise enough to know that if we did let them grow together, we'd find out that "weeds," by God's standards, have their fair worth and role to play in the scheme of things.

I can testify to that. I'm a city boy who this spring decided to plant my first garden. I planted all sorts of respectable seeds, alyssum, zinnias, sweet williams, candy tuft. I've watered them faithfully. Only the candytuft has come up along with all sorts of other green things, which I began to suspect were weeds. Not being an expert on gardens, I've suspended judgment, watered them, let them grow, and studied them on my hands and knees for signs of respectability. And I'm sure now they are weeds. But I've come to know them so well! And, you know, they, too, have blossoms, quite tiny and blue and purple and pale orange. They're not so foul. They're quite fair and admirably persistent creatures of God.

SEVENTEENTH SUNDAY IN ORDINARY TIME

Matthew 13:44–52, Robert Louis Stevenson

Buried Treasure

Jim Hawkins gave the oilskin package to Dr. Livesey. He had found it among the belongings of Billy Bones, an old seadog, who had recently died at the Inn managed by his parents not far from the seaport of Bristol. What with several piratical looking fellows spying upon the Inn, Jim suspected the package might be important and so had delivered it to the doctor and another trustworthy citizen, Squire Trelawney. Upon their opening the mysterious parcel, they found an account book and a map of an island with indicators of buried treasure! " 'Livesey,' said the Squire, 'you will give up this wretched practice at once. Tomorrow I start for Bristol. In three weeks' time—three weeks! . . . we'll have the best ship, sir, and the choicest crew in England. . . . We'll have favourable winds, a quick passage . . . and money to eat—to roll in—to play duck and drake with ever after.' "[37]

How predictable human nature is. Jesus, 2,000 years ago, described in a parable how a person might react upon discovering buried treasure: he would rejoice and sell all that he had to possess it. And here, in Robert Louis Stevenson's tale *Treasure Island* we behold two otherwise proper English gentlemen behave with the same excitement and haste to retrieve a surprise fortune that will make them forever content.

Of course, the hidden treasure Jesus ultimately spoke of was the kingdom of heaven, something spiritually precious, while Stevenson's story deals solely with literal treasure, literal doubloons buried beneath the sand of some Caribbean island. Or does it? Could it be that Stevenson's story is also about the kingdom of heaven? Could it be that, while he seduces us to follow his account of the good ship Hispaniola's quest for literal gold, he has hidden within the very text of his story a reference to the spiritual treasure Jesus speaks of? I think he does.

But before I give you a map to that buried reference, we shouldn't ignore the spiritual insights we can derive from the very surface of Stevenson's tale—for example, the revelation of how little difference there is between the "gentlemen" and the "pirates" in the story. For despite the fact that the former come across as respectable, law abiding chaps and the latter as ruthless, greedy denizens of the underworld, the "gentlemen" turn out to be just as ruthless and remorseless about acquiring stolen goods and more effectively so, since they're shrewd enough to monopolize all the guns and resources to protect their advantage! As a metaphor, the Hispaniola becomes nothing other than every Ship of State upon which the have's occupy the high and mighty steering stern and the have-not's the lowly fo'c'sle in a perpetual state of tension over who will ultimately possess the wealth of the world.

But getting back to that reference Stevenson has buried within his text through which we might catch a glimpse of the treasured kingdom Jesus would have us seek. My map indicates you will find it in chapter 29 where captured Jim Hawkins observes the pirate crew vote to depose Long John Silver as their leader. They record their vote on the blank side of a scrap of paper torn from the last page of the Bible. After viewing the note, Long John tosses it to Jim (and to you and me) for on its reverse side are verses from the last chapter of the book of Revelation, which tells of that bejeweled City of God outside whose gate all the greed, deceit, and violence displayed in *Treasure Island* must be left behind if we are ever to have access to the truly "treasurable" experience of a world where grace and mercy and solidarity reign supreme!

EIGHTEENTH SUNDAY IN ORDINARY TIME

Matthew 14:13–21, Flannery O'Connor

Temples of the Holy Ghost

The child was in for a long weekend. Two older cousins had come to stay on a brief leave from their convent school. They arrived in their brown convent uniforms but were no sooner in the house than they took them off and put on red skirts, loud blouses, lipstick, and high heels and walked around, "always passing the long mirror in the hall slowly to get a look at their legs."[38] They also put on airs, being 14 years old. But the younger child was unimpressed. She thought they were ugly and skinny.

Her mother was at a loss as to how to entertain them; she knew no boys their age. The mischievous child suggested they invite Alonzo, the 18-year-old driver who delivered the girls from school. Alonzo was a stout fellow who "chewed a short black cigar and . . . had a round sweaty chest that showed through the yellow nylon shirt he wore." The girls screamed in protest.

Then the cousins set about washing their hair and putting it up in curlers and calling each other Temple One and Temple Two amid a gale of giggles. When asked to explain, they told the child's mother how Sister Perpetua had given them a lecture on what to do (and here there were more giggles) if a young man should "behave in an ungentlemanly manner with them in the back of an automobile." Sister Perpetua said they were to say, "Stop, sir! I am a Temple of the Holy Ghost!" And they laughed uncontrollably.

The child, who was a belligerent Catholic, living as she did in a southern town of the 1950s where Catholics were few and therefore serious about their identity and values, "sat up off the floor with a blank face. She didn't see anything so funny in this." Nor did her mother. "After all," said she, "that's what you are—Temples of the Holy Ghost."

I find that line such a refreshing reaction to the giddiness of the cousins in Flannery O'Connor's tale "A Temple of the Holy Ghost." I mean, we've lived for so long in a modern world whose favorite refrain seems to be: it ain't necessarily so; the things that you're liable to read in the Bible; it ain't necessarily so.

We live in an environment that finds it ridiculous to accept as fact anything that's not scientifically verifiable, an intellectual climate that winces at any notion we could possibly be the products of a personal Creator or have immortal souls. And so we waver. We concede that many of the particulars of our faith tradition may not be "necessarily so." We even join in the ridicule.

But not that Southern Catholic mother! She seems to realize that if we concede everything, then all we're left with are tons of verifiable information about nature and the stars and biology and evolution that tell us nothing about what we really want to know— like who we are and what speaks to us from beyond death. To her all such information is so much amusing hypothesis compared to the "facts" our souls crave to hear: that we are indeed Temples of the Holy Ghost and that all nature is nothing less than an astounding sacrament, reflective of the Creator who authored us and guides both us and our children toward an unfathomable destiny.

The Bible contains many episodes such as today's passage from Matthew that describe the miraculous nourishment of people who were starving to death. Their intent includes a reminder that the Church, despite its failings, remains the keeper of a miraculous cupboard that contains the only truths that can satisfy our insatiable souls.

NINETEENTH SUNDAY IN ORDINARY TIME

Matthew 14:22–33, Robert Frost

Persistent Expectation

When I began my Christian journey on the sea of life, God was in his heaven and all was right with the world. I believed all that I was taught within the sheltered environment of my parochial community. There was indeed a heaven above populated by saints and by angels, too, many of whom walked invisibly beside us as guardians. Jesus was divine. He died but rose again and was present within the tabernacle, signaled by a red lamp. The world was full of meaning for me. It had a personal beginning and a celestial destiny.

Life was full of metaphor: every highway might remind me of my path to God, every breeze of the Holy Spirit, every rose of the blossoming center of the universe, every bridge of my potential passage from current depression to a better world ahead. In this perception of reality I was not unlike generations of Christians before me going back beyond the Middle Ages. To question my faith perception of the universe and its destiny never occurred to me— until I ventured beyond my parochial environment, came into contact with "modern" and more recently "postmodern" ideas.

Now the "modern" ideas had been around a long time. You could trace them back at least to the 1600s by which time scholars had begun to question everything we once took for granted. For instance, where exactly is heaven if that blue sky is only an ozone layer beyond which there extends a mute universe of stars that require a million lifetimes to reach? Where exactly is hell if all beneath our feet is geologically explainable? And did Jesus really exist or are we all just whistling Dixie? Don't the many discrepancies in the Bible prove it to be all fabrication? And a bridge is simply a bridge, isn't it? Why burden it with any significance beyond what common sense dictates?

Of course, you've undergone this process as well as I. And today's Gospel is descriptive of where and how we find ourselves. Like the disciples in their fragile boat, we may feel adrift in a universe that seems deprived of all meaning, subject to media challenges that hit us like so many head winds, tossed about by waves of doubt. But don't worry! For our Gospel reading and any true poet will tell you that fashionable skepticism is ultimately no match for faith. Where a merely rational man sees nothing but an empty horizon, faith expects to see Christ striding on the waters.

Robert Frost celebrates this expectant faith of ordinary folk. In his poem "Neither Out Far Nor In Deep" he remarks how, when ordinary folk visit the seashore,

> All turn and look one way.
> They turn their back on the land.
> They look at the sea all day.

There's "obviously" nothing out there and if they'd only turn and look landward there would be so much more to see: houses, trees, hills, shops, boardwalks. But despite its apparent emptiness, it is the sea that captivates them:

> The land may vary more;
> But wherever the truth may be—
> The water comes ashore,
> And the people look at the sea.
>
> They cannot look out far.
> They cannot look in deep.
> But when was that ever a bar
> To any watch they keep?[39]

TWENTIETH SUNDAY IN ORDINARY TIME

Matthew 15:21–28, Saint Thérèse of Lisieux

Assumpta est Maria

There is a prevalent impression that men are the primary movers and shakers in biblical history. It all starts off with Adam. Then along come Noah, Abraham, Jacob, Joseph, and Moses to name a few. Even in the New Testament women seem to have only a support role. But is that impression accurate? The feast of the Assumption certainly celebrates a woman whom biblical history could not do without.

And there are other episodes in which a woman changes the course of history—for instance that Gospel account in which a Gentile woman approaches Jesus and asks him to cure her daughter. Jesus says, "I was sent only to the lost sheep of Israel." In other words, "My mission rests within the boundaries of my

Jewish community; I have neither mandate nor time to attend to the needs of a Gentile." Now a quite rational Gentile male might have accepted the logic of Jesus' snub and walked off hat in hand. But, thank God, this Gentile was a woman with a fast comeback— something to the effect: "Is it too much to spare a few crumbs off the table of your privileged few?" And Jesus dissolves. He's charmed by the woman's audacity into expanding his mandate to embrace an alien right there on the spot—and thereby sets a precedent the early Church will remember when it, too, wavers between preaching only to Jewish compatriots or widening its scope to embrace the entire world. That woman made a difference.

Nor is that the first time a woman compels Jesus to extend his boundaries. Take the marriage feast at Cana. Jesus is there as a guest; he has not yet gone public. His hosts are out of wine but Jesus is passive. According to his heavenly Father's schedule, his "hour had not yet come." This makes no sense to his mother. In effect, she says, "I'm not sure what schedule your Father's on, but there's a family here that needs a miracle right now!" Jesus had no comeback to match the authority of that demand; so he succumbed to her appeal to launch his redemptive career prematurely and magnificently.

The Old Testament itself is laced with similar incidents. Check the account of Rebecca's deception of old Isaac to insure that the descendants of Jacob and not of irresponsible Esau acquired a leading role in the redemption of the world. Check those stories about the courage of Tamar, Rahab, Ruth, Deborah, Bathsheba, Esther, Judith, and the New Testament's account of Mary's unhesitant "yes" to God. In every crisis, while the men folk duck for cover, a woman emerges to take the initiative and advance the well being of the human race. And in the process, the Feminine becomes a perpetual metaphor of God's own relentless Spirit, working to create life and cosmos out of chaos.

This makes one wonder why women are still so often treated like second-class citizens. It's an enigma that certainly puzzled our latest Doctor of the Church, Saint Therese of Lisieux. In her remembrances of a trip to Rome when 15 years old she writes in her autobiography:

> I still cannot understand why women are so easily excommunicated in Italy, for every minute someone was saying: "Don't enter here! Don't enter there, you will be excommunicated!" Ah! poor women, how they are misunderstood! And yet they love God in much larger numbers than men do . . . . One day when we were visiting a Carmelite monastery, not content with following the pilgrims in the *outer* galleries, I advanced into the *inner* cloisters, when all of a sudden I saw a good old Carmelite friar at a little distance making a sign for me to leave. But instead of going, I approached him and showing him the cloister paintings I made a sign that they were beautiful. He . . . smiled at me kindly and left. He saw he was not in the presence of an enemy.[40]

TWENTY-FIRST SUNDAY IN ORDINARY TIME

Matthew 16:13–20, Bertolt Brecht

Primacy

I remember being astonished at the size of St. Peter's Basilica in Rome—not only of the whole building but also of the detail within it. For instance, the holy water fonts were about the size of large bathtubs. But what impressed me most of all was the size of the mosaic letters that ran around the upper walls of the place. "THOU ART PETER," they proclaimed in Latin, "AND UPON THIS ROCK I WILL BUILD MY CHURCH AND THE GATES OF HELL SHALL NOT PREVAIL AGAINST IT." You can easily understand why that text was chosen by the architects for such prominent display. For

one thing, this was the pope's Church. And then, in the context of
the Protestant Reformation during which the place was built, what
better way to underscore the now questioned authority of the
papacy than by mounting those words in letters several yards high
around the interior?

Indeed, there was more trouble brewing! Before the basilica
was even completed, the authority of the Church came under even
greater pressure. The age of science had begun. Instruments like the
telescope in the hands of a Galileo revealed the earth to be not the
center of the universe but a pebble orbiting around a minor star
amid billions of other stars. This news scared churchmen more than
the Reformation. Galileo's findings seemed to contradict the Bible's
description of the universe and demanded papal defense of the
Bible's authority and astronomy.

Bertolt Brecht in his play *Galileo* portrays the then Pope
Urban VIII resisting such advice. "I will not set myself up against
the multiplication table. No! . . . This man is the greatest physicist
of our time. He is the light of Italy, and not just any muddle-head . . .
I do not want a condemnation of physical facts. I do not want to
hear battle cries: "Church, church, church! Reason, reason, reason!"[41]
According to Brecht, this pope was obviously no fundamentalist.

But it wasn't the multiplication table or Galileo's facts that
worried the pope's advisers. After all, Galileo's facts had been confirmed by the Papal Observatory. "No," they effectively said, "it's
the doubt those findings will create in everyone's mind. If the movement of the sun around the earth becomes open to doubt, where
will it all end? People will question everything: the divine right of
kings to rule, the superiority of aristocrats, the laws curtailing free
enterprise. And beyond such political and economic principles, will
they not begin to question the truth of scripture, the authority of
the Church, the existence of God, all moral values? And then, where
will society wind up?"

You can see those advisors were not just bullheaded cranks.
In a way, they were prophetic, because in the aftermath of Galileo

came not only political revolution but, more ominously, the manipulation of science by leaders who bestowed upon us the technologically advanced warfare of the twentieth century—plus a few other goodies, like smog. So the pope gave in and suppressed Galileo's works (for which the Church has recently apologized).

But thanks to such crises we do have a clearer understanding of just what kind of authority the papacy and Church represent. It has less to do with the workings of nature and a lot to do with faith, hope, and love. It has to do with insisting on the Sermon on the Mount and the possibility of miracles in the face of skepticism. It has to do with insisting upon the primacy of service and beautiful behavior over greed, of mercy over vengeance, of trust over paranoia, of vitality over inertia, of poetry over a bull market, of the immortal worth of every child brought into this world. It has to do with behaving like a Rock upon which the craziness of self-righteousness, racism, gender discrimination, despair, ignorance, economic injustice, and militarism must forever break and recede. And it has a lot to do with practicing what it preaches.

TWENTY-SECOND SUNDAY IN ORDINARY TIME

Matthew 16:21–27, Lewis Carroll

How she longed to get out of that dark hall . . .

Have you not had the experience of waking up in the wee hours of the morning and wondering where you are? You think, "What time is it?" You look at the illuminated dial of your watch and read, "Three o'clock." Your eyes probe the darkness for a familiar piece of furniture and finally you relax, knowing precisely where you are in time and space. Or perhaps for ever so brief a moment you think you have woken in some other room out of your past—say the guestroom of some friends—and you say, "Oh my gosh! I've overslept my nap. I'll be late for dinner." And then you realize with much relief that you're not in any such chamber you once inhabited but in this one, here and now.

What's going on during that process? Coming out of a deep sleep, we are at first confused, in a fluid state of mind. Things have not yet become immobilized in space and time. Then gradually memory comes to our rescue, helps us identify that mirror, that ceiling, pick up the sound of familiar traffic on Highway 12—and the fluidity gives way to fixation.

Note the sigh of relief. The whole process suggests that we are never quite comfortable except when we reside within a known, predictable, habitual frame of reference. Wary of too much mystery, concerned over our survival, we grow up constructing a very selective state of consciousness. We learn to recognize only those things and people and circumstances and memories and expectations that affirm us. We ignore things that tend to negate or confuse us. In other words, we dwell in a kind of corridor of consciousness where, because it's so familiar, we need exert little thought. We think we are wide-awake, whereas we are only awake to a very selective sample of reality.

In this we're not unlike Alice in Wonderland who found herself in a long, low hall down either side of which were locked doors "and when Alice had been all the way down one side and up the other, trying every door, she walked sadly down the middle, wondering how she was ever to get out."[42] Why sadly? Because it's not healthy to remain perpetually within a corridor of habitual consciousness, oblivious of God's wider world beyond.

That's certainly what the Bible as well as all true literature, art, music, and even science would say. That's why the Bible in its richest passages is all about enticements, apparitions, angels, and Christ himself inviting us to follow them out of narrow mindedness into a fuller vision and experience of reality. I mean, there's old Abraham and Sarah, grown old and resigned amid the familiar furniture of imperial Babylon, being summoned to "go to the land

I will show you, where despite your being old and childless there awaits you a progeny more numerous than the stars in the sky." There's anxious Jacob, seeking refuge amid the familiar tents of his kinfolk, who sees a stairway on which angels ascend and descend—who wake him up to the holiness of everything around him. There's Lazarus standing at the exit of his tomb, to whom Jesus says, "Come forth, come out of your deadly containment to experience the fullness of life that awaits you in every sunrise you ignore, at every Eucharist you attend absentmindedly."

Of course, venturing beyond our habitual state of mind and vision isn't easy. Our precious egos cling to the customary. We resist even as in today's Gospel Peter resists Jesus' invitation to acquire a better understanding of what Jesus is all about. And Jesus rebukes him in no uncertain terms. After all, having just bestowed on Peter the keys to the kingdom of heaven, he expected the poor fellow to use them!

TWENTY-THIRD SUNDAY IN ORDINARY TIME

Ezekiel 33:7–9, Flannery O'Connor

I Have Appointed You Watchman!

The role of moral and cultural watchman, as described in today's first reading, seems more often to be taken up by poets and story writers in our day than by those ordained to play that role. Or at least their poems and stories seem to communicate better than formal encyclicals. Flannery O'Connor was certainly one of the more forceful literary watchmen of the twentieth century. She was acutely aware of the erosion of Christian faith and values in modern times. She recognized the cultural amnesia affecting the politics, economics, media, and churches of America. And she confronted it with a blend of belligerence and wit that make her stories the equivalent of shock therapy. One is about George Poker Sash, titled "A Last Encounter with the Enemy."

O'Connor describes Sash as a man who "had forgotten history and he didn't want to be reminded again."[43] He was a one hundred and four year old Confederate general, though if the truth were know, he had been probably no more than a foot soldier. But it would be no use asking him because he didn't remember the war at all. "He had forgotten the name and face of his wife and the names and faces of his children or even if he had a wife and children, and he had forgotten the names of places and the places themselves and what had happened at them." And good riddance to it all—except for one event of his recent past: the premiere of a nostalgic Civil War film. As a survivor of the Civil War the promoters wanted him on stage prior to the film's debut and he still savored that moment, although he was miffed over being yanked out of the spotlight and led back to his seat before he could say, "I'm glad to be here at this preemy with all these beautiful guls!" That pretty much sums up George Poker Sash's level of consciousness at 104.

According to Flannery O'Connor, it also summed up our own civilization's level of consciousness by the late twentieth century! Our culture has been around for a long time. Our roots are traceable to the Bible and to Greco-Roman thought. But of late we seem to be as willfully ignorant of the fact as General Sash. Even last week's tragedies, epidemics, movies, or map of the world might as well be carted off with last week's trash for all the relevance they have for people this week. So much of our energy seems dedicated to insuring the obsolescence of what we make today so that we can forget it for something new tomorrow. We have no time to reflect, but what's there to reflect on? After all, we are so much more advanced than prior ages. What can the past possibly have to say to us who anticipate discovering the meaning of life sometime tomorrow in the discovery of some "new" Gospel, some sure-fire therapy?

But can we really persist in willful amnesia forever? General Sash wasn't able to. Forced again to play the guest of honor at his aging daughter's college graduation, he sulked upon the stage. He didn't like these quasi-liturgical events with their long commemorative addresses. And now something strange happened. It was as if a hole had opened in his head and the music and addresses began to enter into the dark places of his brain.

> He heard the words, Chickamauga, Shiloh, Johnston, Lee . . . the old words began to stir in his head as if they were trying to wrench themselves out of place and come to life. . . . He felt that he was running backwards and the words were coming at him like musket fire. . . . the entire past opened up on him out of nowhere and he felt his body riddled in a hundred places. . . . He saw his wife's narrow face looking at him critically . . . he saw one of his . . . sons; and his mother ran toward him with an anxious look; then a succession of places . . . rushed at him as if the past were the only future now and he had to endure it.

To be a Christian means never to forget, always to remember. To be a Christian means to extricate oneself from the shallowness of the modern marketplace and gather around the ancient table of the Lord every Sunday to ponder the words of our forbears, to open our souls to the Word made Flesh and know once more who we are and why we are and where we're going. To be a Christian means to have enough cultural depth not to wind up like General Sash whom his daughter awaited after the graduation, not realizing that—thanks to the thirstiness of his boy scout attendant—General Sash was now sitting in his wheelchair—a corpse in a long line leading up to a Coca Cola machine! Symbol, perhaps, to Flannery O'Connor of our vending machine culture—all soda, no substance!

TWENTY-THIRD SUNDAY IN ORDINARY TIME
TOPICAL: UNFINISHED SYMPHONIES

Marcel Proust

While driving down Highway 12 last week I tuned in to 102.1 FM
to catch some classical music and heard the announcer promoting
a contest. I forget the details but the first listener who would call
in and identify the musical clue would win something. He then
played a few bars of the mystery score. I recognized it immediately
(who wouldn't?). It was the memorable melody of Schubert's
Unfinished Symphony.

Flash back! I am a freshman at a Christian Brothers' High
School. I am sitting at a desk among 40 other boys in Brother
Raymond's music appreciation class. It wasn't as though we students
didn't already appreciate music. We were all fans of Benny Goodman,
Artie Shaw, and Spike Jones and the City Slickers. But Brother
Raymond's task was to make us appreciate classical music and
the buzz of a piece of chalk past one's ear gave evidence of his
frustration—for every once in awhile he would pivot from whatever he was writing on the blackboard and hurl that little white
missile with the speed of a bullet at some barbarians in the back of
the room who, assuming he didn't have eyes in the back of his head,
were exchanging comic books.

I myself was philistine enough to find the class boring.
But then one day as I was pondering whether to have an éclair and
Coke or jelly donut and 7 Up for lunch my attention was suddenly
drawn to the record Brother Raymond was playing. It was Schubert's
Unfinished Symphony. I sat transfixed. The melody infiltrated my
being and lifted me to nameless and imageless levels of delight,
love, peace. I was delivered for ever so lovely a moment from my
adolescence. The classroom receded from view as that spiral of
notes carried me aloft like a gentle whirlwind from which vantage

point I could sense the reality of a world beyond my hitherto petty interests.

In Marcel Proust's *In Search of Lost Time,* Charles Swann has a similar experience. He was reluctantly present at a salon party in Paris when the musicians began a piece of music he had first heard a year before—a sonata by Vinteuil. When he had first heard it, a phrase within the piece seemed to hold out to him "an invitation to partake of intimate pleasures of whose existence, before hearing it, he had never dreamed, into which he felt that nothing but this phrase could initiate him."[44]

Until that moment "he had long since ceased to direct his course toward any ideal good, and had confined himself to the pursuit of ephemeral satisfactions . . . . More than this, since his mind no longer entertained any lofty ideals, he had ceased to believe in (although he could not have expressly denied) their reality. He had grown also into the habit of taking refuge in trivial considerations, which allowed him to set on one side matters of fundamental importance." But now, like a confirmed invalid whom a change of air or a new course of treatment seems to have relieved of his malady, "Swann found in himself, in the memory of the phrase he had heard . . . the presence of those invisible realities in which he had ceased to believe." He was conscious once again "of a desire, almost, indeed, of the power to consecrate his life."

To him the music he heard seemed to emerge from "an immeasurable keyboard . . . on which . . . some few among its millions of keys, keys of tenderness, of passion, of courage, of serenity . . . have been discovered by certain great artists who do us the service . . . of showing us what richness, what variety lies hidden, unknown to us, in that great black, impenetrable night of our soul." Or to put it more simply: the piece of music put Swann (even as Schubert's *Unfinished Symphony* put adolescent me) in touch with the very Ground of his being—the God whence all of us arise as potentially great and forever unfinished symphonies.

And where will you find such music within the Bible? Why almost everywhere. But you will especially find it in the first letter of John where a simple phrase like "Everyone who loves is begotten by God . . . for God is love" has been for 2,000 years nothing less than music to our ears.

TWENTY-FOURTH SUNDAY IN ORDINARY TIME

Sirach 27:30—28:7, Matthew 18:21–35

Set Enmity Aside

The Bible is a wise old document. It is the product of 2,000 years of inspired observation of human behavior and attitudes and it hasn't missed much. When it comes to the way human beings react to real or assumed offenses committed against them, the Bible records three kinds of response—two that are more common and one that's quite unusual.

Response 1: Blast away! This is the one Lamech (in Genesis) was partial to, as reflected in his famous remark: "If Cain is avenged sevenfold, then Lamech seventy-sevenfold," or 490 times to be precise. In other words, if someone cuts me, I'll kill him. Even if he's but 12 years old, I'll kill him." Lamech's is the simple approach to compensation. In modern times his attitude translates into: "You shoot one of our guys, we'll bulldoze your village to rubble; you cross my property line uninvited, I'll nuke you—and no jury will convict me—or at least no jury should." It's well to remember that something of this Lamech sentiment festers in each of us. I feel something of it, every time I watch my home team pile up the score against our NFC nemesis—whose name I will not mention.

Response 2: Hey! Take it easy! Don't get mad, get even. Be rational. An eye for an eye, a tooth for a tooth. Let the punishment fit the crime. Keep things proportionate, otherwise passion will beget passion (a Hatfield and McCoy approach to life) and injustices will simply multiply until no one is safe. If you feel you've been taken advantage of, stick to agreed-upon rules and procedures, estimate the appropriate damage and seek that plus the cost of litigation—no more, no less. This is how the lawyers of our parish make their living and until the millennium arrives we'll continue to need their services.

Response 3: (Millennial?) This response will be found in the Gospel in remarks (if I may paraphrase) like: "If anyone strikes you, turn the other cheek; if anyone would sue you or take your coat, let him have your shirt as well. Forgive your brother not once, not seven times, but 70 times seven times—or a minimum 490 to be precise.

This latter response is not as popular as Response 1 and 2, but the Gospel challenges us to try it. Why? Because obviously Response 1 is insane and decimates the innocent along with the guilty. And it will boomerang every time, for if the whole family of a man who offends you is a fair target for your wrath, what's to prevent the survivors of that family from making your whole nation fair game? And isn't that what history books are sadly all about? As regards the more moderate Response 2, I think it was Mahatma Gandhi who said all that has ever resulted from an eye for an eye resolution to human disputes is a world full of blind men.

So, says Jesus, why not give creative, imaginative love and forgiveness a try, if only because it, too, can have its boomerang effect—in that you, too, may be forgiven all the offenses you have committed and tend to overlook in your relentless quest for compensation from the rest of the world around you.

TWENTY-FIFTH SUNDAY IN ORDINARY TIME

Matthew 20:1–16, Somerset Maugham, Gabriel García Márquez

Grace: The Best of Surprise Endings!

Too often we forget that God is not all we think or imagine Him to be. For example, ever since Moses met God on Mount Sinai we've thought of Him as party of the first part to a contract in which we are party of the second part. In other words, we imposed on God the quid pro quo way we wary human beings have of doing business. Perform and you will receive an appropriate reward! Five ounces of virtue placed in the tray of the scale will be matched by a corresponding weight of blessing in the other. That's how we operate. Therefore, that's how we assumed God must operate—even as the workers in today's parable expected their employer to act.

But along comes evening and the parable presents us with a surprise ending! God—as revealed by Jesus in this story— extricates Himself from the quid pro quo bind in which we've trapped him. He breaks loose to reveal Himself to be a God of absolute generosity, of boundless grace. For God is no mere employer. He's a Father dealing with us as His children, not as mere wage earners. And as such He will operate so much more intimately, generously, extravagantly.

What Jesus is saying in this story to his religious contemporaries is this: "If you want to persist in viewing God as a quid pro quo deity, then labor away in measured ways through the heat of the day for a measured recompense. But if you're open to the surprising fact that God is really so much more grand and gracious than that, then line up to enjoy his generosity and in the process perhaps learn to release all that generosity buried deep within your very self. The choice is yours as to which God you wish to deal with."

Of course, this parable of Jesus set a trend. Acts of extraordinary generosity often conclude stories of Christian culture as in

Somerset Maugham's tale "The Know-All".[45] It's about an Asian Indian merchant name Mr. Kelada traveling by liner to Japan. The narrator shares a cabin with him and can't stand him, because he never stops chattering about everything with the air of an expert. And then one evening at dinner the subject of pearls comes up. Kelada boasts there's no fake pearl he can't detect. A bet of 100 dollars is placed. The shy wife of a wealthy American, Mr. Ramsey, happens to be wearing a string of pearls and Kelada is asked to evaluate it. He concludes it's probably worth 30,000 dollars. The American smiles. His wife bought it in a department store for a mere 18 dollars! Everyone enjoys Kelada's discomfiture.

He himself blushes and asks to look at it again. A smile of triumph spreads over his face and he's about to speak, when he catches a desperate appeal in the eyes of the American's wife. He stops, admits he was indeed mistaken, that the pearls are a very good imitation, worth no more than 18 dollars. He also pays out the 100 dollars.

Later that evening, the narrator is present in their shared cabin when a note arrives from Mrs. Ramsey returning the 100 dollars—for the pearls were indeed real and cost much more than 18 dollars, though her neglectful husband would never know it, thanks to Kelada's noblesse oblige.

Or again there's the story by Gabriel García Márquez called "Balthasar's Marvelous Afternoon"[46] about a poor artisan who makes a most palatial birdcage for the son of the wealthy Jose Montiel— only to find out the father knew nothing about the order. Upon its delivery, Montiel therefore makes a terrible fuss and denies he had any obligation to pay for it. The boy falls to the ground, weeping with disappointment. Balthasar then holds out the cage to the boy who rises to embrace it. The father becomes even more vehement and insists Balthasar take it back. Ignoring the father, Balthasar tells the boy to keep it and then goes off to a local tavern to celebrate the most delightful experience he has ever had.

Three stories, one by Jesus and two by modern writers, all of which end with a surprise! And what is the surprise? That beyond our chilly world of quid pro quo, of strict accounting, something warm, something truly divine can happen: namely, God; namely, grace.

TWENTY-SIXTH SUNDAY IN ORDINARY TIME

Philippians 2:1–11, Frank O'Connor

Let's Play Hide and Seek!

Brother Arnold and Brother Michael were Irish Trappist monks. They lived under a rule of silence and custody of the eyes. This meant they were to keep their eyes cast down when not focusing on their work and thereby avoid distraction. Given these circumstances neither knew very much about the other.

Brother Arnold managed the monastery cattle and Brother Michael took care of the stables. One day Brother Arnold went to the stables to retrieve something he had lent Brother Michael. But Brother Michael was nowhere to be seen. Arnold then heard a sound from within one of the stalls. He looked in and saw an embarrassed Michael holding his hands behind his back. Brother Arnold sensed he was unwelcome and quickly backed out of the place. All that day he wondered what Michael had been up to.

The next day Brother Michael signaled Brother Arnold to follow him into the stable. He closed the door and then mischievously pulled a newspaper from his long sleeve. It was the *Irish Racing News*. At the sight of it Brother Arnold's face broke into a broad smile. So that's what Brother Michael had been up to! By way of sign language wiry Brother Michael indicated he had once been a jockey and had other forbidden racing journals stashed away to keep up with the sport.

This discovery of Brother Michael's little vice added a bit of spice to Brother Arnold's life. Amid all the pious faces of his confreres he had discovered a naughty and therefore "human" one—and it somehow released his own repressed humanity. He had to reciprocate. So the next day when Brother Michael came into his office, Brother Arnold closed the door and reached above it to take down a bottle from behind a loose stone. He handed it to Brother Michael who raised the bottle to his lips and then coughed in surprise. It turned out to be an excellent beer. Brother Arnold had now revealed a peccadillo of his own to match Brother Michael's and from then on the two men became fast if still silent friends. "They no longer had any secret from one another. Each knew the full extent of the other's little weakness and liked him for it."

This parable by Frank O'Connor called "Song without Words"[47] seems to tell us that it's only by mutually admitting our peccadilloes, our weaknesses that we shall ever achieve true community—because such honest sharing can evoke from deep within us that sense of mutual identity and compassion which alone can make of us not a collection of strangers but a family at last.

A code of silence and custody of the eyes still rules our behavior in this great monastery we call the world, despite Saint Paul's admonition in today's second reading that we look out not solely for our own interest but also for those of others. A woman at work next to me breaks down in tears; I look away—while she apologizes, saying, "It's nothing. I'm quite all right, thank you." That has to stop. It's imperative that I show I care and that she feel she can share whatever it is that makes her cry—partly for her own consolation and partly because discovery of her hurt can be for me what Michael's secret became for Brother Arnold: "a window . . . into his own loneliness"—awakening within him that bittersweet feeling that makes us want to embrace the whole of a fragile humanity.

TWENTY-SEVENTH SUNDAY IN ORDINARY TIME

Philippians 4:6–9, Victor Hugo

Doors

In today's second reading Saint Paul pleads with us to ponder—for contagion's sake—whatever is true, honorable, just, pure, lovely, and gracious. If anything is every bit of that, it's the behavior of Jean Valjean in the course of Victor Hugo's *Les Misérables*. Of course, Jean did not start off behaving true, honorable, just, and so on. He started off very bitter when, upon his release after 19 years in prison for stealing a loaf of bread, he found all the doors of local inns closed to him. Like many a homeless person he finally settled upon a bench in the cathedral square, when an old woman asked him what he was doing. He angrily replied, "I've knocked at every door. . . . I've been turned away everywhere."[48] The woman pointed to the house next to the cathedral. "Have you knocked at that one? . . . Then do."

Jean did knock and found himself in the home of the bishop where he received not only food and a bed for the night but was shaken by a rare experience of mercy, for, when Jean was later arrested for having desperately stolen the bishop's silver plate, the bishop told the police Jean hadn't stolen it at all; the bishop had bestowed the silver plate upon him as a parting gift.

As a consequence of the bishop's gracious generosity toward him, Jean himself went on to become a gracious man. We find him later under an assumed name, Monsieur Madeleine, living as a successful and enlightened businessman who shared with his employees and the whole community the benefits of his enterprise. He even became mayor and community problem solver.

But a shadow fell across his path, that of the sinister, relentless Inspector Javert, who sensed there was something shady about Monsieur Madeleine. Javert had been tracking Jean Valjean for years

for some other assumed offense and felt sure Madeleine was his man.
Madeleine knew this and was concerned. So you can imagine his
surprise when one day Javert came to him, confessed his suspicions
and apologized, announcing that the real Jean Valjean had been
found and was about to go on trial in Arras. Monsieur Madeleine
was shaken. What to do? If he kept quiet, he would never have to
worry again. Javert and the courts would forever think Jean Valjean
was down there in Toulon on a prison ship and Madeleine (the real
Jean Valjean) could retain his new identity, remain a resource to his
community. He pondered this option even as his body carried him
toward Arras and the other man's trial.

 The court was already in session. Known to be a public
figure, Madeleine was ushered into a small chamber. "This is the
judges' room," said the usher. "The door with the brass knob leads
directly into the courtroom." Madeleine's "eyes fell on the brass
handle of the door . . . . Beads of sweat formed on his scalp and
rolled down his temples." Once again he stood before a door
behind which truth, honor, justice, purity, loveliness, graciousness,
in a word, Christ, awaited him. He hesitated, backed away, retreated
down the corridors by which he came, then paused and returned
to the judges' chamber. "Suddenly, and without knowing how
it happened, he found himself standing at the door. He seized the
handle with a convulsive movement and the door opened. He was
in the courtroom." Then in the mildest of voices he said, "Gentlemen
of the jury, you must acquit the accused. I must request the
court to order my arrest. I am the man you are looking for. I am
Jean Valjean."

 What metaphorical doors have you had to—perhaps
reluctantly—open in the course of your life to become all those
things of which Saint Paul writes: true, honorable, just, pure, lovely,
gracious? More lie ahead because that seems to be how God works.
And if you recall how Christ in John's Gospel identified himself as
"the Door," that may encourage you to anticipate beyond every
crisis, every portal you confront an experience akin to that of Jean

Valjean. Valjean, having identified himself on the other man's behalf, declared before an astonished court: "You who are here present . . . find me deserving of pity, do you not? For myself . . . I think I am to be envied."

***

TWENTY-EIGHTH SUNDAY IN ORDINARY TIME

Matthew 22:1–14

Il Sacro Speco (The Holy Cave)

About 40 miles east of Rome you run up against the mountains around Subiaco, the region to which a young Saint Benedict retired around 500 AD. to live in solitude and contemplation. An older hermit showed him a cave high up on the cliff of a canyon and there he remained until, drawn by appeals of others, he emerged to found the present monastery at Subiaco and the Benedictine order which went on to civilize Europe's barbarian ancestors.

The original cave can still be seen within the walls of the precariously perched priory that was built around it ages ago. It has been incorporated into a series of three chapels dating from before 1100 AD. There is a large upper chapel from which a stone stairway leads down to the chapel built around the cave itself. Each chapel is a jewel. There are arches and slender columns, a marble altar covered with gold, blue, and crimson mosaics. But most overwhelming are the frescoes dating from as early as 700 AD, which cover every square foot of wall and ceiling.

Obviously the monks who created these chapels were not content only to hear the Gospel. They needed to see it happening all around them. And so they painted the walls and ceilings with splendid impressions of Gospel events. The upper chapel portrays the whole climax of Christ's life, from his entry into Jerusalem, the kiss of Judas, the flight of the disciples, his Crucifixion, the meeting with Mary Magdalen in the garden, His confrontation of doubting

Thomas, to His ascension into heaven. There it is in reds, blues, purples, silver, and gold. And then there are iconic images of Mary and saints. In the lowest chapel there's even an image of Saint Francis, painted from life when he visited the place in 1223. It's tucked behind a corner at shoulder level and when you stumble upon it in all your vulnerability, his wide open, gracious eyes look right into your soul.

Well, as if the art weren't enough, when my wife and I recently visited this treasure there was a wedding in the upper chapel. In other words, we were lucky enough to experience the place not as a mere museum but as an environment alive with faith and love. It was as though all those frescoes were hardly relics of the past but beautifully present participants in the current event, beaming down with eyes strangely alive upon the equally beautiful bride and groom, family and friends—who were also beautifully attired.

Bellezza! Beauty! That's what summed up for me the whole experience of that place and moment. Beauty. And after all, isn't that what religion is ultimately about: becoming beautiful, perceiving and creating beauty everywhere, behaving beautifully and not just puritanically? And then I shuddered—for, standing there amid all that beauty dressed as I was in the khaki trousers, sports shirt, and hiking boots of your standard American tourist, there came to my mind that Gospel about a wedding feast and I expected someone at any moment to approach me like the king in the parable and ask, "My friend, how is it you came in here not properly dressed?"

And I thought, "By golly, I've got to acquire a change of wardrobe. Not only literally but spiritually. I've got to divest myself of all the sourness and whining and grinding of teeth, the resentments, anxiety, excuses—the things that perpetually mute my beauty. I've got to get more joy, faith, love, vision, grace—in a word— more beauty into my life if I am ever to become eligible to enjoy the world of Christ so beautifully reflected here within this Sacro Speco of Subiaco."

TWENTY-NINTH SUNDAY IN ORDINARY TIME

Isaiah 45:1, 4–6

Thus Says the Lord: I Am in Charge!

The prophet in today's first reading lived in Babylon around 540 BC. He was one of the many Jews who, after the destruction of Jerusalem, were resettled to dwell under the thumb of the Babylonian monarch. Possibly he knew the Jewish songwriter who composed that subversive Psalm 137: "By the streams of Babylon we sat and wept when we remembered Zion."

He was also no doubt attentive to what passed for the media in those days, because he soon learned of things stirring in distant Iran. A young king named Cyrus had come to power and was scoring one victory after another over neighboring kingdoms. In 546 BC his armies had reached as far west as present day Istanbul. This raised our Jewish prophet's hope. King Cyrus was on a roll and wouldn't be satisfied until he swallowed up the Babylonian empire as well. And once he did, considering his liberal policies, he would certainly allow Jews to return to their homeland and rebuild their temple.

The prophet therefore went about telling his fellow Jews in oracles (like the text for today) to rejoice over Cyrus's victories, because Cyrus was God's chosen instrument working on behalf of Israel. To make the situation more current, imagine a rabbi imprisoned in Dachau, upon hearing of General Patton's breakthrough in Normandy and his sweep across France in 1944, speak of the American general as God's anointed: "Subduing nations before him . . . opening doors before him and leaving the gates unbarred: for the sake of Jacob, my servant Israel, my chosen one."

The prophet's point is that despite the suffering we endure (much of which we bring upon ourselves), there is a providential God who guides our destiny. Ultimately, it's not tyrants or nature or what comedians used to call the fickle finger of fate that will determine our future, but a God who works in unexpected ways to insure that the stock phrase "And they lived happily ever after" will be our epitaph.

I can testify to this providence, having just returned from a three weeks tour of Italy. My wife and I planned the whole thing: car rental, itinerary, hotel reservations, and so on. But as the day of departure neared, I grew apprehensive. For starters, on our arrival at Milan we were to drive 250 miles to Perugia. "Why," I wondered, "did I ever decide to do that?" I mean, after 20 hours without sleep, to wander around a strange airport looking for the car, then venture out onto strange freeways around a major city, approach tollbooths wondering which gate was legitimate! What must I have been thinking of? And imagine how much more nervous I would have been had I realized I didn't know how to put a Fiat Punto in reverse! And then there was the ATM worry: would it accept my card? It didn't at first because, much to my panic, the keyboard showed numbers only and I remembered my PIN by a four-letter word. "Now which number would G be?"

Worries, crises—yes, but by the time the trip was over, how superfluous my worries appeared, because at every point along the way they were dissolved so easily by the view from my grandmother's birthplace overlooking the Adriatic or the art of Perugia or the splendor of Ravello or the Greek temples of Paestum. Indeed, the whole trip became for me a metaphor of life. Worries, crises sure! These are the inevitable experience of any fragile human being, but in the end the wonders of God's providence do prevail. And if we could only stop anticipating the worst, if we could learn rather to anticipate the revelations that lie ahead, how much more sublime an experience life and even death would be.

THIRTIETH SUNDAY IN ORDINARY TIME

Matthew 22:34–40, Lewis Carroll

Only He Who Hesitates Is Lost

Alice was bewildered. After falling down that rabbit hole, nothing she experienced conformed to the norms she knew. Animals talked and were ill mannered. She tried to reorient herself by reciting the multiplication table, but it kept coming out: 4 x 5 = 12, 4 x 6 = 13. Her own size changed from tiny to tall and back again. Caterpillars were condescending. She felt absolutely lost and wished desperately to find her way back to her familiar world of Victorian absolutes. So when she saw a Cheshire Cat perched in a tree, she plaintively asked, "Cheshire Puss . . . . Would you tell me, please, which way I ought to go from here?"[49] The Cat grinned and said, "That depends a good deal on where you want to get to" Frustrated, Alice replied, "I don't care much where." "Then it doesn't matter which way you go," said the Cat.

Sometimes we, too, feel lost like Alice. We're so dependent on familiar guidelines, things like longitude, latitude, road maps, catechisms, words that mean this and not that. We like to know precisely where we are and where we're headed—because we don't like being lost. Yet Jesus says in Matthew: "He who loses his life will find it." And in this Jesus was but an echo of the God who said to Abraham: "Leave your country and your kin and your father's house and go to the land I will show you." God didn't say where that might be, and the admirable thing about Abraham was that he didn't ask. He simply pulled up stakes and stepped into the unknown.

Saint Francis reflected that same sense of abandon. You know the story of how, whenever Francis came to a crossroad, he had Brother Juniper whirl round and round until he lost his balance and fell flat on his face! In whatever direction Juniper fell, that's the road Francis took.

Perhaps it was the spirit of Saint Francis that induced me to exercise such abandon on my recent trip to Umbria. I, too, am a worrier like Alice. I've been taught to follow a map to feel secure, be it a philosophical, ethical, or topographical map. And so, approaching the Italian town of Perugia, I became nervous—because Perugia is a mountain town, its narrow streets ascending to its center by twists and turns that resemble on a map a plate of linguini. Our hotel was at its apex and before ascending, I closely consulted Perugia's map and then ventured up what seemed the right street—and made a wrong turn. I had no idea where I was. And when my meandering led me to a tunnel (which looked to me like the mouth of hell), panic struck. Despite the honking of cars behind me, I backed off and returned to the maze behind me. Only when my wife saw a sign saying "Centro" did I yield to its enticement and let the car make its roller coaster way up and down and around—until, by golly, we exited into Perugia's top piazza—right outside our hotel!

For two more days (after excursions into the countryside) I went through similar trepidation negotiating Perugia's labyrinth, yet always by totally different twists and turns reached our hotel. Then it hit me: God was teaching me to wing it! "Throw the map away," he said. "Go with the flow." And thereafter, approaching Perugia, I'd laughingly say, "I wonder which route the car will take this time?" Instead of a nightmare, driving into Perugia had become fun.

Today a scribe, who was possibly confused by all of the major and minor do's and don'ts of the Torah, asks Jesus to help him sort them out. In effect, Jesus says, "Lay that map aside! Live with abandon! Simply love God and your neighbor with all your heart and mind and soul and you'll find your way. Indeed, you will become a way for all the world to follow."

THIRTY-FIRST SUNDAY IN ORDINARY TIME

Matthew 23:1–12, Kenneth Grahame

Climb Aboard

> Grown up people really ought to be more careful. Among
> themselves it may seem but a small thing to give their word
> and then take back their word . . . . But with those who
> are below them, whose little globe is swayed by them, who
> rush to build star-pointing alhambras on their most casual
> word, they really ought to be more careful.[50]

This was the complaint of the young narrator of "The
Magic Ring" in Kenneth Grahame's *Dream Days,* a collection of
reflections about the plight of siblings who lived under the super-
vision of "Olympian" adults on an English estate a century ago.
This particular complaint was aimed at one of the adults who
had noted in the newspaper the arrival of a circus in town and
suggested the family go on Wednesday.

Now for children, whom walls seemed to cramp and stifle,
the imperative thing was "to escape into the open air, to shake
off bricks and mortar and to wander in the unfrequented places of
the earth." A circus promised just that: bareback riders on ponies,
clowns, calliope music! Needless to say, the children dreamed about
nothing else, day and night. The narrator especially dreamed of
riding a coal-black horse round and round the circus ring in pursuit
of "a princess all gauze and spangles, who always managed to keep
just one unattainable length ahead."

But when Wednesday dawned, the grown ups had forgotten
about that casual reference to a circus. There was talk instead of
a scheduled adult garden party that very afternoon—leaving the
children with pangs of disillusionment. To their protest the grown
ups replied "Some other time, dear!"—a "stale, worn-out old

phrase" that the children nevertheless had come to expect whenever the grown ups promised anything. Little Harold, however, let out a wail. "He had drawn his check on the Bank of Expectation, and it had got to be cashed then and there; else he would yell, and yell himself into a fit." But all to no avail. For the children "the earth was flat again—ditch-riddled, stagnant and deadly flat."

So off they went to throw stones at any little critter that showed its head by the wayside—until they heard the rattle of a passing cart and turned to see the funny old man who drove it to town every day. They called him funny because "he was sad and serious, and said little, but gazed right into our souls, and made us tell him just what was on our minds at the time, and then came out with some magnificently luminous suggestion that cleared every cloud away." It didn't take him long to fathom their depression and so he said his wife had sent him on an errand: "But never mind . . . . Suppose we go off to the circus?"

"Wings of fire sprang from the old mare's shoulders." Off they whirled to town, and late that evening the children went to bed with their imaginations full of march music and bareback riders and hilarious clowns, gorgeously costumed, forever stumbling and suffering ridicule yet always getting the best of it in the end.

Don't you find there a parable of our own situation in this world, especially around election time? We, too, down through the centuries have been given so many promises by statesmen, inventors, ideologues, all offering us some panacea (along with a lot of fine print) guaranteed to cheer us up once and for all, but always letting us down because they lack the capacity of that funny man to gaze into our souls and fathom our profoundest needs. But every Sunday along comes that great chariot—the Church—which Dante saw in his *Divine Comedy* to convey us liturgically out of a cramped and hypocritical world into a magical realm of faith, hope and love— to entice us (as our little narrator put it) "to escape into the open air . . . to wander in the unfrequented places of the earth." Why not climb aboard!

THIRTY-SECOND SUNDAY IN ORDINARY TIME

Matthew 25:1–13

Behold, the Bridegroom! Come to Meet Him!

People of ancient times saw the sun not as a mute star burning impersonally some ninety three million miles away, but as mother earth's heavenly bridegroom, destined to arrive every springtime to wed her once more, to summon forth all the life that lay dormant within her throughout the dark winter months. And they celebrated this annual wedding with songs whose echoes still resonate from that little read Old Testament book called the Canticle of Canticles or Song of Songs or Song of Solomon.

It's a little read book because, growing up as—at least we once did—in so puritanical a culture, phrases like the following made us squeamish:

> My beloved is all radiant and ruddy . . . . His lips are lilies,
> distilling liquid myrrh . . . . His legs are alabaster columns,
> set upon bases of gold.[51]

> Behold, you are beautiful, my love . . . . Your eyes are doves
> behind your veil. . . . Your lips are like a scarlet thread . . . .
> Your cheeks are like halves of a pomegranate.

But, of course, the folks of the Mediterranean were not as repressed as we are. They were exuberant; they proudly multiplied such images to express their emotions.

Now if you read the Song of Songs closely you will hear the bride, our mother earth, lamenting the absence of her brilliant groom during the dark winter months:

> Upon my bed at night, I sought him whom my soul loves—
> I sought him but found him not . . . I slept, but my heart was

> awake. Hark! my beloved is knocking . . . I arose to open
> to my beloved—but my lover had turned and gone. . . .
> I sought him, but found him not.

Well, after all, it's wintertime, isn't it, and all she will find if she
wanders outdoors will be those night watchmen, the stars.

But inevitably the dark season passes away. Come
springtime, the energizing sun begins to rise more radiantly upon
the eastern horizon. The earth is touched by his power:

> Behold, he comes, leaping upon the mountains, bounding
> over the hills. There he stands . . . gazing in at the windows,
> looking through the lattice.

You've had that experience, haven't you, of the early morning
sun peering through the blinds of you bedroom? And he speaks
to his earth bride:

> Arise, my love, my fair one, and come away; for lo, the winter
> is past . . . . The flowers appear on the earth . . . . The fig
> tree puts forth its figs, and the vines are in blossom; they give
> forth fragrance.

The marriage of heaven and earth has been consummated.
And, oh, how the sun admires his bride the earth! She is described as
a garden enclosed; her teeth are like a flock of ewes, her belly like a
heap of wheat encircled with lilies. What a marvelous description of
what happens when sunshine and our fertile planet get together!

Fortunately, Israel preserved this beautiful metaphor and
stretched it to describe Israel's longing for God and God's ever-
passionate commitment to Israel as his "garden enclosed." And
today's parable? Doesn't it seem like a further allusion to the Song
of Songs, except that here it is Christ, the light of the world, whom
we await to wed humanity, to invite us all to participate in a marriage banquet, an everlasting Eucharist in which mutual love will be

such that—as the Song of Songs puts it—many waters cannot quench it nor floods extinguish it. But beware! Don't let your store of faith diminish to the point where, when you hear the cry "Behold, the bridegroom," you've got no energy left to join the party.

THIRTY-THIRD SUNDAY IN ORDINARY TIME

Matthew 25:14–30, Edward Robinson

Miniver Cheevy, Child of Scorn

Apparently the master in today's parable had little confidence in the initiative of the servant to whom he gave but one talent to invest. Perhaps he saw in the fellow too much of a dreamer in the negative sense—a fellow suspicious, if not cautious of the world around him and therefore prone to watch TV or sit through movie matinees. In other words, he was inclined to live in a fantasy world as opposed to the harsh daylight of the world of business, interaction, and abrasions.

In other words, the fellow had already chosen prematurely to bury his very gift of life, so what was the point of vesting him with more than the least responsibility? He's obviously just another Miniver Cheevy, of whom Edward Robinson says:

> Miniver Cheevy, child of scorn,
>> Grew lean while he assailed the seasons;
> He wept that he was ever born,
>> And he had reasons.[52]

Of course, people who recoil from the difficulties of work, relationship, and the imperfections of our world and institutions tend to get high and mighty. To muffle the voice of conscience they justify their recoil from life; they rationalize, point out with eloquent clarity the silliness, the pettiness, and injustice of the world around them. They see themselves as too special to put on overalls and get rid of that junk that's been piling up in the garage for several years or do the dishes. The fact that they can't find a free hanger in the closet makes them feel imposed upon, justifying their retreat to the sofa where they can drift off into some golden age where their true qualities might be evident to all.

> Miniver loved the days of old
>> When swords were bright and steeds were prancing;
> The vision of a warrior bold
>> Would set him dancing.

But that's about as far as Miniver could get. For all his admiration of this more heroic, Technicolor image of himself, he still had no gumption. Caught between detachment from the demands of current reality and a notion of himself as nobler, adventuresome, superior to his prosaic peers, he could only remain plaintively inert.

> Miniver sighed for what was not,
>> And dreamed, and rested from his labors;
> He dreamed of Thebes and Camelot,
>> And Priam's neighbors.

But is Miniver Cheevy any different from you and me? Haven't we to some degree buried our talent, repressed the particular gifts God has given us to make a difference in this world? Oh, sure, we try to snap out of it, try to become eligible for the master's "Well done, my good and faithful servant." We wake up one morning, saying, "This is it! I'm going to break out of this rut and impress the world around me with real deeds of derring-do! I'm going to stop complaining, stop being mesmerized by television. I'm going to become an energized person." Then we open the refrigerator to find we're out of eggs, sigh, and grow wearily philosophical again.

One should beware of lingering too long on such a tread-mill of high aspiration followed by a deep sleep, considering how:

Miniver Cheevy, born too late,
　　Scratched his head and kept on thinking:
Miniver coughed, and called it fate,
　　And kept on drinking.

But not to worry! For even as the season gets darker, making spiritual hibernation even more attractive, the Church stands by to disturb our lethargy, explode our escapist fantasies with that wonderful liturgical device called Advent and the Christmas season! Yes, indeed! Pretty soon an angry John the Baptist will come shouting through the dormitory, telling us all to wake up! And angels will follow on his heels to hustle us off to Bethlehem to rekindle the embers of last spring's Pentecost.

LAST SUNDAY IN ORDINARY TIME
OUR LORD JESUS CHRIST THE KING

Matthew 25:31–36, Nathanael West

When Did We See You a Stranger?

In 1933 Nathanael West published a novel called *Miss Lonelyhearts*.[53] It's about a New York newspaperman who writes a daily feature under the pen name Miss Lonelyhearts—("Are-you-in-trouble? Do-you-need-advice? Write-to-Miss-Lonelyhearts-and-she-will-help-you"). It was an idea cooked up by the paper's editor, Shrike. Its apparent purpose was to offer advice to the readers of the metropolis, but its real purpose was to increase circulation; to capitalize on human suffering. Everyone at the paper saw the column as a joke—even the fellow assigned to play Miss Lonelyhearts. Then the letters started coming in.

"Dear Miss Lonelyhearts—

I am in such pain I don't know what to do sometimes I think I will kill myself my kidneys hurt so much . . . I have 7 children in 12 years and ever since the last 2 I have been so sick. I was operatored on twice . . . I cry all the time it hurts so much and I don't know what to do. Yours respectfully, Sick-of-it-all."

"Dear Miss Lonelyhearts—

I am sixteen years old now and I don't know what to do and would appreciate it if you could tell me what to do. When I was a little girl it was not so bad because I got used to the kids on the block making fun of me, but now I would like to have boy friends . . . and go out on Saturday nites, but no boy will take me because I was born without a nose— although I'm a good dancer . . . and my father buys me pretty clothes. I sit and look at myself all day and cry . . . . What did I do to deserve such a terrible bad fate? . . . Sincerely yours, Desperate."

The godless editor Shrike thought the letters hilarious. After so many years in journalism dealing with human suffering on a global and local scale he had become cynical. The futility of human existence amused him. Life was obviously one cruel joke; so why not laugh instead of cry? So he would lean over Miss Lonelyheart's shoulder while he typed and nag: "The same old stuff . . . . Why don't you give them something new and hopeful? Tell them about art." Then he would sneeringly dictate platitudes like: "Do not let life overwhelm you. When the old paths are choked with the debris of failure, look for newer and fresher paths." But over time Miss Lonelyhearts himself began to react differently. The more he read the letters, the more he felt their pain—and soon every band aid reply he wrote seemed sacrilegious.

Individuals living out there in the tenements of New York or com-
muting on subways; or children anonymously revealing anxiety
over domestic violence—how could he ever adequately respond to
the unique pain of their misspelled petitions?

Then he began to realize his letter writers were not so much
looking for solutions to their immediate problems. In the terrible
privacy of their anguish what they wanted more than anything else
was someone to care. What they were pleading for was love—not
just the kind you get from a perfunctory letter, but also a love that
reaches right down to the soles of your feet and guarantees that you
are not expendable, that your life has been no joke. He trembled to
think that they were asking of him something that seemed beyond
his human capacity to give—a love that was divine. And yet the
summons was so attractive: this call to transcend himself and the
Shrikes of this world, to become a truly human being, a saint.

In today's Gospel, Christ the King makes such proactive
sensitivity the ultimate criterion by which humanity will be judged:
"Come, you who are blessed by my Father. . . . For I was hungry
and you gave me food . . . a stranger and you welcomed me . . .
ill and you cared for me!"

THE COMMEMORATION OF ALL THE FAITHFUL DEPARTED

2 Maccabees 12:43–46, Paul Horgan

"It Is Good and Holy to Think of the Dead Rising Again"

"I never saw such color as this year; the trees are like lamps, with
the light coming from within."[54] So thought Cleotha Powers in
Paul Horgan's story, "The Peach Stone," about the passing peach
orchards as she and her husband began the long drive from their
ranch amid the tumbleweed of New Mexico to transport the body

of their two-year-old daughter (contained in a sandpapered wooden box) to the family burial plot in Cleotha's girlhood town of Weed. The orchards reminded her also of how as a girl she used to catch up the peach petals by the handful, crush them, and wrap them in a handkerchief to place in her bosom so that she might smell like peach blossoms—and of how her girlfriends used to say that if you held a peach stone in your hand long enough, it would sprout. But then no one wanted to hold a peach stone that long to find out and so they would laugh about it. But Cleotha believed the saying—and she especially believed it now in her bereavement.

Indeed, ever since she woke up that morning a spell had come over her. She had done all her weeping the night before. And now she never wanted to merely look at anything anymore; she wanted to see. She wanted to watch for any signals of something grand and eternal within the ordinary contours of reality—so much so that instead of relaxing for the journey ahead she felt herself leaning forward in the back seat, reaching with her eyes beyond the windshield to single out things like this unusual beauty of the peach orchard. Or look! In that next orchard—that dead tree! But still there's that little swarm of green leaves on its top branch. And what's that dazzling light on the road—like a ball of diamond light that danced and quivered so far ahead? Could it be a daytime star, sent to guide them? That it might only be sunlight reflected off the metal of an oil truck made no sense to her because, as I have said, Cleotha was trying to see! She wanted to catch a glimpse of where her daughter, whose inert form lay beside her, had gone.

Hasn't that been the question that has preoccupied bereaved human beings ever since the dawn of our species? Our appetite for life and love, our insatiable curiosity bridles at the thought of our being ultimately and forever confined within a space of but six feet by two. We want to know! And it was this need to know that now possessed Cleotha. Or to put it theologically, she was operating now out of faith and hope—that extra pair of eyes with which sorrow and love endow us.

And so the most consoling thing she finally saw, once she and her relatives and friends knelt by the burial plot halfway up Schoolhouse Hill, was a boy, a late scholar, coming down the hill from the school. He was framed in sunlight and she couldn't help but notice his wonder, his own reaction to death, to the people kneeling mournfully around a grave. So young, so innocent of death, and yet discretely coming down the hill, that edge of sunlight around him, shying away from the mystery and yet large eyed with a hunger to know—to know in ways his schoolhouse will not teach him. And Cleotha found in his respectful curiosity so potent a confirmation of her own and all humanity's need to know, to envision that "undiscover'd country from whose bourn no traveler returns" that she cried out, "I believe, I believe" and she said it "as if she were holding the peach stone of her eager childhood in her woman's hand."

I've been holding a peach stone in my closed fist for ten years now—come this April. I've been leaning forward, not just looking but trying to see amid the unfolding wonders of spring signals of an even greater spring to come—somewhere beyond the windshield of my mind. And what I'm precisely looking for is the gradually unfolding presence of the son I knew, who I hope has had the patience to wait for me upon whatever path he has been traveling since his death, so that together we may continue what— ten years ago—was just beginning to be fun.

MOTHER'S DAY

Henrik Ibsen

Peer Gynt (Peer being Norwegian for Peter) is playwright Henrik Ibsen's model of a very modern gentleman.[55] Even in the late 1800s Ibsen could foresee in Peer Gynt the "rugged individualism" that would characterize our current society. Peer Gynt lived for himself

alone. In his youth he was always the hero, the loner, the Clint
Eastwood of his fantasies. When it came to women, his attitude was
to love them and leave them. He literally ran away from any commitment to others. His motto was "I've got to be myself!"—that
narcissistic refrain echoed in so many modern songs like "I gotta be
me!" and "I did it my way!"

The folk of his provincial village therefore found him
obnoxious. Only his mother and a farm girl named Solveig could
see through his egotism to his hidden potential to become a uniquely
generous and beautiful human being. But he had no time for their
sermonizing. He had to do "his thing" regardless of how much it
hurt other people. And so he left Norway to make his fortune.

Like the other robber barons of his day, he became an
entrepreneur. It didn't matter what he sold, so long as he acquired
the wealth, power, and independence to do as he pleased. He
engaged in the slave trade. He shipped idols to China and, to both
ease his conscience and add to his income, he shipped bibles as
well. In other words, he played it both ways—the way the tobacco
industry might invest in medical research to develop a lucrative
remedy for lung cancer.

Failing at commerce, he later decided to become a guru,
a regular Elmer Gantry, to exploit the gullibility of simple folk.
Later still, he opts to become an ivory tower scholar, to "float like
a feather on History's tide." Even amidst shipwreck (as he returns
an older man to Norway) his creed of "me first" remains evident
in his remark to another survivor clinging to his raft: "Let go your
hold—she won't take two."[55]

But by the end of the play Peer Gynt has second thoughts
about living for oneself alone. Broken and weary he plucks an
onion from the undergrowth of a forest clearing and he reflects:
"Why, you're simply an onion and now, my good Peer, I'm going
to peel you." And so, layer after layer he peels away his careers
of scholar, guru, entrepreneur, playboy—all the games he's played
in the pursuit of self-interest—until beneath them all he finds no

center, no core at all. There's nothing that's solid, generous, beautiful, real—no sublime self that he can be honestly proud of.

And so he returns to the Solveig he left so long ago, who (as a symbol of maternal Wisdom) has prayed for him and loved him for the Christic potential she saw in him. He kneels before her, crying, "Where was I? Myself—complete and whole? Where?" And the patient Solveig replies, "In my faith, in my hope, and in my love." In other words, his true Self had always been retained by her within her heart (as in a tabernacle) until such time as he could return and humbly retrieve it and become all she always knew him to be—a uniquely gifted child of God.

And (it being Mother's Day) may we not say the same of every mother here today? For what is a mother but someone who, regardless of how much her child may have gone astray or whatever an impersonal world may think of him or her, retains within her heart a conviction of that child's unique beauty and potential. Which is why, when all else fails, we can always return to her as a kind of sacrament of God's own maternal commitment to each of us. This is why we may in some way say of every mother: "Hail, full of grace! The Lord is with thee. Blessed art thou among women."

MEMORIAL DAY

Wichita

Some months ago, passing through St. Leo's parking lot, I saw a bumper sticker that said something like "I served on the Wichita." Immediately my mind went back to a November day in 1937 when I stood beside my father at the Philadelphia Navy Yard and beheld something simply wonderful to the eyes of a nine year old boy: the launching of the heavy cruiser, the U.S.S. Wichita. Philadelphia had always been a Navy town. The Navy began there under John Barry and sailors were always seen striding up Broad Street. And it was always Navy we boys rooted for during the annual Army-Navy game played in town. Army gray was an unwelcome visitor. It was Navy blue that we admired.

And so you can imagine the thrill I felt as I stood there along the port side of the Wichita (named for the only city in Kansas I will never forget)—its sleek hull rising above me upon greased ways; signal flags dancing in the breeze. And then there was a burst of champagne and slowly the great ship began to slide, the timbers fell away; it picked up momentum and gracefully settled into the embrace of the Delaware River as into its proper element—and I went home feeling: "The U.S.S. Wichita will always be my own special ship."

It was only much later that I finally traced the owner of the bumper sticker to Bill Barber at a Men's Club dinner. He had served on the Wichita as a shipboard marine and was able to lend me its full photographic history. And what a history it was. The Wichita served in nearly every theater of the Second World War, in both the Atlantic and Pacific! But its story ends on a poignant note. After so remarkable a career, the official history says of her: "In 1959 she was sold for scrap to the Union Minerals and Alloys Corporation." And I thought, "How sad!"

And yet I also began to think: "You know, the Wichita was obsolete the very day it was launched," because already naval technology was changing. The aircraft carrier would soon become queen of the fleet (Pearl Harbor proved that). And then there would be nuclear this and nuclear that to make even battleships relics to be tied up beside Old Ironsides.

Nor was it just naval technology that was changing; it was our whole age of innocence. Back then we were not possessed of a highly critical mind. We were patriotic, trusted our institutions, had no doubts about the justice of our causes or the structures of our Church. Our horizon stopped at the boundary of our home-town whose axis was called Main Street. Our historical horizons went back to Valley Forge, our cultural horizons to Hiawatha and the bleachers of Ebbets Field. But it was a time about to change under the influence of so many things like the G.I. Bill and mobility and electronics, which would disintegrate and reconfigure not only our politico-economic world but our Church as well.

And so it's no wonder that on days like Memorial Day some of us aging folk, weary of modern change, meditate not only about past wars but the end of an era. And yet isn't it about time we widened the scope of Memorial Day? I mean, isn't it time for us to remember not only those simpler days of our youth but the whole of our lives to date—the growth, the insights, the mellowing tragic experiences (which I never anticipated as I stood beneath the prow of the now-scrapped Wichita)—experiences that have made us deeper persons, less gullible, more global in our sense of citizen-ship, less racist, more compassionate—ripe with a ripeness called wisdom—a wisdom we owe to new generations lest they pay an even higher price in a nuclear age for international, racial, ethnic, class, inter-religious, and interpersonal animosities which we now know, thanks to the Holy Spirit, to have been always absurd?

FATHER'S DAY

Seamus Heaney

Of Bicycles and Swings

As I think about Father's Day, two experiences come to mind that sum it up for me. The first has to do with my eldest son, Adam. I have this pleasant flashback to those afternoons when I introduced him to the rope swing suspended from an oak tree in our backyard in Baltimore. He was a frisky two and a half years old and enjoyed the swing immensely, judging by the squeals he emitted as he went sailing off into the sun-spangled foliage and then came sweeping back down over and over again.

Of course, I was pushing him and what an ineffable plea-
sure that was. I would place him in the swing's saddle and then
slowly draw him back to the height of my chest and then give him
a good shove and off he'd go, to return again to the height of my
chest and then to my brow as I applied enough pressure to get him
as high as the physics of a swing would allow. After that it only took
the gentlest of touches to keep him arcing ever so gracefully while
I sang to the rhythm of it all: "The swing goes up; the swing comes
down; your toes touch the sky; your bottom the ground."

There was something about the experience that entranced
me. It seemed to embody the very essence of fathering. For what
does a father do but launch his child into life as if upon a swing—
introducing him to a world that's a blend of danger yet delight? Nor
do you want to spare him the danger lest he never know the delight.
And all the while you back him up with a music set to the rhythm
not so much of a swing but of your heart.

And there you are again, whenever he returns, not to abort
his flight but only to send him gently off again until one day, like a
bird out of its nest, he sails off to become the beautiful person you
already knew he was. For they do take off eventually as Seamus
Heaney testifies in his poem "The Swing":[56]

> Sooner or later,
> We all learned one by one to go sky high . . .
> Toeing and rowing and jack-knifing through air . . .
>
> In spite of all we sailed
> Beyond ourselves and over and above
> The rafters aching in our shoulderblades,
> The give and take of branches in our arms.

With my now deceased younger son Philip, my memorable
experience was different. I recall the day I helped him first ride
a bicycle. Phil was always a bit behind his brother and peers in

mastering the skills of play. And so, when his brother and I escorted him to the big Mall in Washington, D.C., I did not expect him to mount the contraption and sail off blissfully competent the way Adam did. That's why I picked a level, grassy field, figuring there would be fewer abrasions to treat.

And sure enough, every time he climbed aboard and I gradually let go of the seat to leave him to the mercy of gravity, he wobbled and wobbled and down he went with a clatter and a moan and a gripe. Only upon the fifteenth try did he zigzag away until he reached his cheering brother a good 50 yards off—and grew smaller in my vision, leaving me with a memory that has made my life worth living.

It's as simple as that. Two metaphors of fatherhood! Launching children into a world where falls are probable but where their victory over gravity (in every negative sense of the word) is also probable as long as you are there with supportive fingertips, which are nothing less than an extension of your heart.

But, again, they do sail far beyond our reach, as in the case of Adam who (much to my admiration and muted concern) now climbs high ladders as a member of the San Francisco Fire Department. As for Philip (figuratively speaking), the last I saw him he was—like the boys in the movie E.T.—riding a bicycle silhouetted against the moon. But—unlike them—E.T.'s spaceship took him away.

Endnotes

1. Charles Dickens, "A Christmas Carol" in *Christmas Books* (New York: Charles Scribers Sons, 1897), p. 70.

2. Frank Norris, *McTeague* (Penguin Books, 1982). All quotations are from this edition.

3. Mark Twain, *The Adventures of Tom Sawyer* (Chicago: World Library Limited edition, Field Enterprises Educational Corporation, 1975), pp. 2–3.

4. Allen Ginsberg, *Howl And Other Poems* (San Francisco: The Pocket Poets Series, City Lights Books, Twentieth Printing, 1968), p. 9.

5. William Wordsworth, "The world is too much with us" in *Wordsworth: Selected Poetry,* ed. Nicholas Roe (New York: Penguin Books U.S.A., 1992), p. 194.

6. W. H. Auden, "For the Time Being" in *Collected Longer Poems* (New York: Vintage Books, Division of Random House 1975). All quotations are from this edition.

7. Anne Porter, "The Ticket" in *An Altogether Different Language* (Cambridge, Massachusetts: Zoland Books, 1994), p.113.

8. Daniel Defoe, *Robinson Crusoe* (New York: Barnes and Nobles Books, 1996), pp. 32–33.

9. John Milton, "Lycidas" in *The Complete Poetical Works of John Milton* (Boston: Houghton Mifflin Company, 1965), p. 147.

10. Melissa Kay, "A Hymn To My Son" (with permission of the author).

11. Seamus Heaney, "Personal Helicon" in *Opened Ground Selected Poems 1966–1996* (New York: Farrar, Straus and Giroux, 1998), p. 14.

12. E. M. Forster, *A Room with a View* (New York: Signet Classic, Penguin Books, 1986), p. 282. All quotations from this edition.

13. William Butler Yeats, "Calvary" in *Selected Poems and Two Plays of William Butler Yeats,* ed. M. L. Rosenthal (New York: Collier Books, Macmillan Company, 1966), p. 194. All quotations from this edition.

14. Flannery O'Connor, "Revelation" in *Wise Blood, The Violent Bear It Away, The Complete Stories* (New York: Quality Paperback Book Club by arrangement with Farrar, Straus, and Giroux, 1992), p. 488. All quotations from this edition.

15. Herman Melville, *Moby Dick* (New York: Random House, 1930), p. 66. All quotations are from this edition.

16. John Drury, *Painting the Word* (New Haven, Yale University Press in association with The National Gallery, London 1999).

17. Kenneth Grahame, "The Fairy Wicket" in *Pagan Papers* (London: John Lane, The Bodley Head, 1898), p. 157.

18. Francis Thompson, "The Kingdom of God" in *Man and God* by Victor Gollancz (Boston: Houghton Mifflin Company, 1951), p. 431.

19. Jonathan Swift, *Gulliver's Travels and Other Writings,* Part II, (Boston: Houghton Mifflin Company, Riverside Editions, 1960), pp. 106–109.

20. Eudora Welty, *A Curtain of Green And Other Stories* (San Diego, New York, London: Harcourt Brace Jovanovich, Publishers, An HBJ Modern Classic, 1991), p. 165 ff.

21. Pius Parsch, *The Church's Year of Grace,* Volume 3, (Collegeville, Minnesota: The Liturgical Press, 1954), p. 224–226.

22. Isak Dinesen, *Babette's Feast and Other Anecdotes of Destiny* (New York: Vintage Books, A Division of Random House, 1988), p. 41.

23. A. N. Wilson, *Paul, The Mind of the Apostle* (New York and London: W. W. Norton and Company, 1997), p. 161. All quotations from this edition.

24. A. E. Housman, "A Shropshire Lad" in *The Making of a Shropshire Lad,* ed. Tom Burns Haber (Seattle: University of Washington Press, 1966), p. 33.

25. Thomas Mann, *The Magic Mountain* (New York: Random House, Inc. Vintage Books Edition, 1969), p. 4–5.

26. Mark Twain, *The Adventures of Huckleberry Finn* (New York: The Modern Library edition, 1993), p. 315. All quotations are from this edition.

27. Anne Porter, "In Chartres" in *An Altogether Different Language* (Cambridge, Massachusetts: Zoland Books, 1994), p. 57–60.

28. Kenneth Grahame, *The Golden Age* (Berkeley, California: Ten Speed Press, 1993), p. 181. All quotations from this edition.

29. John Steinbeck, *The Grapes of Wrath* (New York: Penguin Books U.S.A. Inc., 1992), p. 236. All quotations are from this edition.

30. James Joyce, *A Portrait of the Artist as a Young Man* (New York; The Viking Press, Inc., 1964), p. 158.

31. Gerard Manley Hopkins, "Pied Beauty" in *Poems and Prose of Gerard Manley Hopkins* (Baltimore: Penguin Books Inc., 1953), p. 30.

32. Seamus Heaney, "Digging" in *Opened Ground: Selected Poems 1966–1996* (New York: Farrar, Straus and Giroux, 1998), p. 3.

33. Denise Levertov, "Primary Wonder" in *The Stream and the Sapphire* (New York: New Directions Books, 1997), p. 33.

34. Charles Dickens, *Great Expectations* (New York: Viking Penguin Inc., 1965), p. 164. All quotations from this edition.

35. Isak Dinesen, "The Cardinal's First Tale" in *Last Tales* (New York: Random House, Vintage Books Edition, 1975), p. 23.

36. Evelyn Waugh, *Brideshead Revisited* (Boston: Little, Brown and Company, 1945), p. 86 ff.

37. Robert Louis Stevenson, *Treasure Island* (New York, Viking, A Division of Penguin U.S.A., no date), p. 61 ff. All quotations from this edition.

38. Flannery O'Connor, "A Temple of the Holy Ghost" in *Wise Blood, The Violent Bear it Away, The Complete Stories* (New York: Quality Paperback Book Club, 1992), pp. 236–238.

39. Robert Frost, *The Poetry of Robert Frost,* ed. Edward C. Lathem (New York: Holt, Rinehart and Winston, 1969), p. 301.

40. Saint Therese of Lisieux, *Story of a Soul: The Autobiography of Saint Thérèse of Lisieux,* Third Edition (Washington, D.C.: ICS Publications, 1996), p. 140.

41. Bertolt Brecht, "Galileo" in *The Experience of Literature,* ed. Lionel Trilling (Garden City: Doubleday and Company, Inc., 1967), p. 405 (Scene XI).

42. Lewis Carroll, *The Annotated Alice: Alice's Adventures in Wonderland and Through the Looking Glass* (New York: Clarkson N. Potter, Inc., 1960), p. 29.

43. Flannery O'Connor, "A Late Encounter with the Enemy" in *Wise Blood, The Violent Bear it Away, The Complete Stories* (New York: Quality Paperback Book Club, 1992), p. 142. All quotations from this edition.

44. Marcel Proust, *Swann's Way*, trans. C. K. Scott Moncrieff (New York: Penguin Books U.S.A. Inc. 1957), pp. 245 and 408.

45. W. Somerset Maugham, *The Complete Stories of W. Somerset Maugham*, v. 2 (Garden City, New York: Doubleday and Company, 1953), p. 142 ff.

46. Gabriel García Márquez, *Collected Stories*, trans. Gregory Rabassa and J. S. Bernstein (New York: Harper Perennial, 1984), p. 138 ff.

47. Frank O'Connor, *Collected Stories* (New York: Alfred A. Knopf, 1981), pp. 33–39.

48. Victor Hugo, *Les Misérables* (New York: Penguin Books U.S.A. Inc. 1982), p. 80. All quotations from this edition.

49. Lewis Carroll, *The Annotated Alice: Alice's Adventures in Wonderland and Through the Looking Glass* (New York: Clarkson N. Potter, Inc., 1960), p. 88.

50. Kenneth Grahame, "The Magic Ring" in *Dream Days* (Berkeley, California: Ten Speed Press, 1993), p. 71. All quotations from this edition.

51. All quotations taken from the "Song of Songs" titled "Song of Solomon" in *The New Oxford Annotated Bible with Apocrypha*, Expanded Edition, Revised Standard Version (New York: Oxford University Press, Inc. 1973).

52. Edward Robinson, "Miniver Cheevy" in *The Pocket Book of Verse*, ed. M. E. Speare (New York: Pocket Books Inc. 1940), p. 350.

53. Nathanael West, *Miss Lonelyhearts and the Day of the Locust* (New York: New Directions Paperback, 1962), pp. 169–171.

54. Paul Horgan, "The Peach Stone" in *The Best American Short Stories of the Century*, ed. John Updike (Boston, Houghton Mifflin Company, 1999), p. 224 ff. All quotations from this edition.

55. Henrik Ibsen, *Peer Gynt*, trans. Peter Watts (Baltimore: Penguin Books Inc., 1966). All quotations from this edition.

56. Seamus Heaney, "The Swing" in *Opened Ground: Selected Poems 1966–1996* (New York: Farrar, Straus and Giroux, 1998), p. 400.

About the Author

Geoff Wood holds a doctorate in theology and a licentiate in scripture from The Catholic University of America in Washington, D.C., and the Pontifical Biblical Institute in Rome. He is retired from an early academic career in religious studies and subsequent employment in the evaluation of human services at the national and local levels. Currently, he lives in Sonoma, California, where he continues to offer adult religious education courses at the parish and diocesan levels. He has been writing weekly essays for several Catholic parishes since 1989.

This is the second in the *Living the Lectionary: Links to Life and Literature* series. Year C was published in 2003 and is available from Liturgy Training Publications in Chicago.